TWIN A

AMIT MAJMUDAR
TWIN A

A Memoir

SL/\NT

BOOKS

TWIN A
A Memoir

Slant Books
P.O. Box 60295
Seattle, WA 98160

www.slantbooks.org

Cataloguing-in-Publication data:

Names: Majmudar, Amit.

Title: Twin A : a memoir / Amit Majmudar.

Description: Seattle, WA: Slant Books, 2023

Identifiers: ISBN 978-1-63982-139-6 (hardcover) |ISBN 978-1-63982-138-9 (paperback) | ISBN 978-1-63982-140-2 (ebook)

Subjects: LCSH: Congenital heart disease | Congenital heart disease in children | Children--biography | Autobiography--Asian American authors

In the book of my memory—the part of it before which not much is legible—there is the heading *Incipit vita nova*. Under this heading I find the words which I intend to copy down in this little book; if not all of them, at least their essential meaning.

—Dante Alighieri, *La Vita Nuova*
translated by Andrew Frisardi

CONTENTS

I

BEFORE YOU

You Are Born

LIGHT IS NEW. IT SPRAYS DOWN, white and caustic, right into your eyes. The pressure on all sides, which you have felt your whole life, which grew firmer and firmer as your body swelled and stretched the walls of your mother—that pressure has dropped away, all at once.

Imagine a passenger in a plane, asleep under a blanket, with a sleeping mask on, his ears accustomed to the engine roar the same way yours were to the roar of blood in the womb. Now the cabin rips open. The sleeping mask and blanket fly off. The passenger awakens from dreamless sleep to find himself falling through a blaze of sunlight.

That's what this is like for you—only from your perspective, you're falling in every direction at once. No wonder you're screaming.

Your sense of gravity was always vague because you have never not been submerged. Your down and up used to shift, subtly or drastically, depending on whether your mother walked, or sat at a certain angle with her legs crossed, or laid on her side or on her back. Now you have one fixed Up and one fixed Down.

Hands hold you and pass you about, doctor to resident to nurse, but you don't know they are hands. Hands are new. They are thin, hard, slick, poky. You are too bewildered to process much about hands, much less the suction bulb stabbing your nose, much less the universe, other than that it is foreign and aggressive, one long sequence of invasions and violations.

The water you used to swallow and breathe is gone, replaced with something far less substantial. Air is new: It has no heft. You never had anything but silence inside you. Sound fills your head now, and the harder you cry, the louder it gets. It is coming from a spot very close to your ears, only on the inside, closer than close: Your voice, too, is new.

You are on a cloth now, under a hot lamp. Cloth is new, and startlingly coarse. Your back has never felt anything but membrane, smooth muscle, flowing water, and crème-fraiche vernix. The hot-lamp feels like something you know, but the heat is all in one place, not all around you, as it used to be. This is distance. This is separation.

Your mouth has never been empty before. Your hands seek out your face, the only things familiar from the womb.

This is the moment, with all the inspections complete—ten fingers, ten toes, pinking up nicely—that you're supposed to be handed back to your mother. She would make a hushing sound, instinctively mimicking the womb's blood rush. The pressure of the swaddling, and her steady hold on you, would stop your freefall into the universe outside you.

But that isn't what is happening, because you aren't pinking up nicely. Your body is strangely gray all over. You are being wheeled into a crowd of waiting hands, which descend from above and spider over you. Thin, slippery tubes with needle fangs snake up from the corners of the bassinet and sting you in the crook of your elbow, the crease of your groin. They begin to suck your blood.

Light, breath, voice, distance, and now pain: sooner than expected, your education is complete.

Welcome to the world, son.

You get inspected by people in different uniforms: long white coat, short white coat, bright green surgical scrubs, bright green surgical scrubs with a white coat over them, blue nursing scrubs.

You don't see them very clearly. You have the stunned-blind eyes of a just-born kitten, glassed with ointment. Dark iris and darker pupil seem to fill the thin slit between your eyelids. You blink at these people, slowly, in a way that makes it seem you are studying them back.

What are they looking for? Right now, your doctors hunt your body for any problems that the ultrasound studies, performed before your birth, could not have picked up. The whole team has been briefed about the big problem with your heart. It's that problem which has made them rush you straight from your mother's body to the intensive care unit.

In all of these faces, scholarly excitement overrides, for the moment, compassion. You are a real live Fascinating Case—and the last thing you want to be, in medicine, is a fascinating case. The greater the rarity, the greater the fascination, and the greater the fascination, the greater your suffering.

These strangers are searching for what's sometimes called a "constellation of findings." In that implicit metaphor, every birth defect is a star, and together these disasters form the image of an Archer, a Bear, a Scorpion. The doctors and doctors-in-training scan your body like a night sky. They don't "want" you to have any of these other signs—like *micrognathia*, small jaw, or *hypospadias*, a urethra splayed open in a pink wet fissure along the underside of the penis. But they do want to *find* the signs, if they are there.

This wish—to see in real life the mythical babies of textbook photographs—will lead to conjectural, almost wishful documentation. So the notes on that first day claim your jaw is too small and the opening of your urethra stretches too far. They have searched you so hard they end up finding what isn't there. A list of Associated Defects, memorized off a flashcard when cramming for an exam years before, gets superimposed onto you. In a few days, these other, minor diagnoses will magically evaporate. But the big one will remain, stubbornly, catastrophically, at the heart of you.

Over and over, more often than any of the others, a face pops into your field of view.

Cheeks a little scruffy, dark eyes sunken behind thin-rimmed glasses, poofy blue surgical cap: This stranger is wearing a full body jumpsuit that seems made of paper, and light blue booties over his sneakers, though you can't see those right now. Occasionally, he puts a glowing rectangle to his ear and chatters into it. At other times, he just blinks at your blinking, or lays his Purel-smelling finger on your palm to feel your fingers close around it. You recognize the voice as one you have been hearing in the womb, though then it came through amniotic fluid, muffled. Now it comes through sharp and raw, even though it's a whisper. Two syllables, as he points at his chest: *deh* and *dee*, *deh* and *dee*.

I know exactly what your alternate destiny looks like, without these wires and beeping computer monitors. Every so often over the next few days, I leave the intensive care unit for a different wing of the hospital. I pass the Einstein Brothers bagel kiosk in the glass-roofed too-bright foyer, the gift shop with the angel trinkets, the piano no one ever plays. I arrive at another bassinet, where a second newborn, identical to you, lies sated, sleeping. Your mother lies near this other you, recovering from her Caesarian section and periodically trying to nurse. It's as if the two wings of this hospital exist in parallel universes, one universe benevolent, the other abandoned to chance. I shuttle between the two yous, wary of shortchanging the you I am not with—two newborns in iambic alternation, one unstressed, the other stressed.

That room is quiet except for a classical *raga* in the background, the lyrics Sanskrit and sacred, the volume kept low. The iPod, nested in a speaker, glows. That faraway, unattainable room is full of family members. It pulses with daylight from the swept-aside curtains.

You should be here, too. You are not here. I am writing this to tell you, among other things, why.

Dear Shiv.

I started this out as a letter. I wanted to outline what went on in the first years of your life. I expected to get down a couple of pages I could put in an envelope, in the safe, along with your Social Security card and passport. When you got old enough to ask detailed questions, I figured I could take it out and let you read it—a letter from me now to the future you. Like the events it describes, the writing escaped my control.

> Hook a circuit up in parallel
> and the voltage—
>
> equal, equal—
> is a single miraculous energy
>
> that cannot be created or destroyed,
> only twinned, twinned,
>
> as a life is
> through a pair of umbilical cords,
>
> your mother powerful enough to charge the sun,
> your mother a hemo-electric power plant
>
> illuminating twin cities,
> illuminating my study lamp's
>
> two light bulbs just above my head—
> equal, equal—
>
> floating there like two ideas
> for telling the same story,

one in prose, one in verse:
Twin A, Twin B:

circuits in parallel,
cries from the heart

born from a shock—

I imagine you reading this years from now when you are a man, or maybe still a teenager—whatever age you are when you stop your life's forward motion to inspect, and marvel at, the obstacle course it has been. I know you will want details and explanations, and you deserve them.

Obviously, we plan to be there to tell you in person, but there is no guarantee of that. Even ignoring worst-case scenarios, I worry about the workings of memory. My own, at the very least: I confess I am already losing things. Anecdotes, bit parts, and peripheral characters, how things played out—these elements are already going the way they always do. The experience has been reduced to freeze-frames and elisions, the record of it scratched and skipping. Ten years from now, how much of my memory will still be readable if I don't write this down now?

Fortunately, your mother has a prodigious memory for every last thing. In her memory, the crisis years are clearly ordered, important details and conversations readily called up. So I have written a lot of this relying on conversations with her, and she is vetting these pages as I go, making sure I don't leave out anything important. I came across a study, as I was writing this down, that showed women possess a superior declarative memory compared to men. That means they are better at tasks like "the retrieval of long-term memories of specific events and facts...[and] thus better at remembering family history." Comparing your mother and myself, this is absolutely true.

"Dear Shiv" is how I began this when I intended to jot down some things that weren't in the medical record. My letter grew and grew into what you're reading now, with stories, and poems, and bits of medicine and anatomy, and some places where I'm just thinking things through with you. Not that I claim some great wisdom, some neat takeaway that will make what happened make perfect sense. All I can do is get down the facts of what happened. You live the wisdom. I observe...and take notes.

Suffer, my boy,
no men of wisdom.
You are twenty
times a swami
by surviving.
Let the gurus
cross-legged
sit at the feet
of Swami Shiv.
You teach them: *Courage*
comes from *cor*,
the heart, and *pulse*
means *seed* and feeds
the rock dove's hunger
every April.
Blood is *sang*
and *sanguine* spirits
sing when no one
else is singing,
heartened by
the hush, no tabla
save your pulse.

In a sense, though, this is still a letter. Think of this book—with all its organs and vessels and bones and nerves, with its fables and explanations and anecdotes and poems—as one long fan l;etter from your dad, sent through time.

Who We Were Before We Were Yours

YOUR MOTHER TAUGHT HIGH SCHOOL ENGLISH. The job market hadn't been all that great when she entered it, so she had interviewed in some of the more post-industrial-wasteland parts of Cleveland. She was late to an interview at one school, only in part because the street signs had been stolen off the poles. Once she parked, avoiding the broken bottles, an enormous black dog trotted out of nowhere, trailing a loose length of chain, and waited patiently at her car door. Eventually, he lost either his interest or his appetite and moved along. The principal gave her a tour of the bulletproof glass around his office and spent the rest of the interview persuading her not to take the position.

Her first year, she taught at a charter school for children with attention-deficit disorder and Asperger's—a job very much in keeping with her nobility of character, and she did come home sometimes with stories of charmingly eccentric students expressing their affection for her in charmingly eccentric ways. At other times, the kids were not so charming. She got her first exposure there to the nihilism of adolescent Midwestern males. The first storytelling assignment came back with tale after tale of parents and siblings murdered in cold blood. Diligent concentration, a low crouch over the desk, meant the student was doodling dyslexic swastikas and mutilated bodies. The school had to troop outside when a six-foot-something thirteen-year-old scrawled a bomb threat on the bathroom wall. He was caught quickly enough since he hadn't bothered to disguise his handwriting.

The charter school's administration seemed full of vice-presidents who took home undisclosed sums of state money for performing undisclosed functions. There was also a "sensei" with a mullet who hung out in a room called the "dojo," thus supplying the martial arts theme outlined in the school's charter. "Chef Ben" stopped in for cooking class. One Tuesday, he walked in dragging the lopped-off leg of a deer, which he proceeded to dress and cut into strips, right there in your (vegetarian) mother's classroom. The stink resisted Tide with Bleach. She had to throw out a coat.

During that year, though, we got word from a neighbor of your grandparents about an opening in the English department of my old high school. Mayfield High School was this protective husband's wish come true: suburban (a mile from your grandparents' house, in fact), low crime rate, and colleagues I knew, in some cases personally—one of the math teachers had graduated the same year I had. All that, and they even passed their levies. Her last name was still familiar in that school, and the magic of her handshake did the rest. The very next year, she was walking, every day, the same halls and rooms in which I had first daydreamed about marrying her.

To be honest, there have been moments I have wondered whether I actually daydreamed her into existence. Your mother combines, uncannily, virtues I believed then to be mutually exclusive. I can recall sitting in English class and zoning out during a book discussion (I'm guessing *Silas Marner*) and deciding that my future life partner ought to be an English major, so we could talk about books other than *Silas Marner*. Ah, but she mustn't have that ironic, roll-the-eyes-at-religion outlook that people catch from hanging around in academia too much. She would be Indian, but not Bollywood-Indian, because *that* kind of Indian culture was frivolous and shallow. She should love, as I do, the classical culture of Gods and epic myths. But she also had to like James Bond movies and prefer Connery to all other Bonds. She would be beautiful, of course, but also funny, defying the conventional wisdom about beautiful girls never developing a sense of humor. She would be able to speak Gujarati to my grandmother in India, but at home, she and I would speak unaccented, telepathically elided English.

With typical teenaged self-absorption, I was designing an Ideal Lover by replicating a model: myself. That imaginary wife was just a female twin. Your real-life mother, when I met her, ended up trumping the solipsist's criteria. She ended up being a graduate of the English program at UC Berkeley; a classical Indian dancer who knew more about the epics and Gods (and despised Bollywood more) than I did; a better Gujarati-speaker, with less of an accent; encyclopedically knowledgeable about P.G. Wodehouse; instinctively aware, after I introduced her to the Bond movies, of Connery's ascendancy over all other Bonds; and able to pun in five languages, English, French, Gujarati, Hindi, and Sanskrit—sometimes simultaneously, always effortlessly. I know I didn't daydream her into existence because I never dared to daydream so extravagantly.

We decided early and grew together like trees planted close to one another, our roots and branches laced and interknotted, our trunks in parallel. That's called *inosculation* in botany, and in poetry, it's called *love*. You and your siblings were born of that love, you and Savya our doubled acorn. We knew each other when we were toddlers. After her family moved from Ohio to California, we saw each other very rarely. When we met again as teenagers, I saw her and didn't feel like I had entered the presence of another person. I figured it must be because we had played together as toddlers. Now I realize she slipped instantly and without a ripple into my solitude. How do you enter a bubble without popping it? That was what she did.

Sometimes, years before you were born, I would watch her sleeping, and her face would relax into one of those Chola bronze statues from ancient India you see in a museum. Her sleep radiated intense heat, more heat than any human fever. I would get the eerie sense I had been sent this being as a guide. Zoom out, fast forward—how else did it happen, fifteen years later, that I found myself researching the *Bhagavad Gita* painstakingly, word by word? Where did all that come from, if not from her? I went from a steak-sawing American of Indian ancestry, reading around in various religions, to a vegetarian husband and father, sounding out 2500-year-old Sanskrit verses. Did I effect that transformation on myself? Was this life the natural endpoint of that first-year medical student, aged nineteen, lifting weights and scooping tuna from the tin? I don't deceive myself. I am what I am because of her, just as you are what you are because of her. They say Brahmins are twice-born: I took my second birth through her and the Goddess within her. Never forget you are born of a woman of purity, faith, moral passion, a sense of what is right, a sense of her past and what she sustains.

I have always been a champion daydreamer, and by the time I became a radiology resident at Case Medical Center in Cleveland, nothing had changed.

I picked Case's program partly because all the other hospitals started a half-hour earlier. Daydreaming, though, was more of a noon conference kind of thing. During morning conference, I found it hard to get through the hour without closing my eyes and blacking out entirely. On Tuesday mornings, we got a lecture series on fetuses.

In those years, my roaring twenties, I went into the hospital on three, sometimes two hours of sleep. I used to write mythological epic poems until I heard sparrows. Other residents with shady secret lives had alcohol, or Fentanyl, or an extramarital call room tryst with a hazel-eyed phlebotomist. The *Ramayana* was my addiction. If sleep deprivation can produce the neurological equivalent of alcohol intoxication, I doctored drunk all through residency. I made up for my mythopoetic self-indulgence with a finicky refusal to abuse any substance but English. I still have no idea what beer or wine taste like, smoking horrified me as a form of incremental suicide, and I am one of the few doctors I know who has never used caffeine to get through an overnight shift or a sluggish morning. So the last thing I needed at 8 a.m. was a PowerPoint about congenital defects—slide after ultrasound slide of vaguely fetusoid static.

The doctor who delivered these Tuesday lectures was not himself a radiologist. An elderly Polish obstetrician, specializing in maternal-fetal medicine, he knew more about fetal ultrasound than anyone in our department. Because he didn't actually supervise our training, he never surprised us with spot questions to catch us napping. In fact, he couldn't grade us in any fashion, so I felt free to zone out. How could I not? His hangdog eyes with irises of gray Eastern European sky, his impossibly fuzzy images. . . . That voice always sounded as exhausted as I felt, uttering after almost every case: "Thees ees, unfortunately, not compatible with life." That refrain remains one of the few things I remember from his lectures, driven into me by repetition. He condemned so many of the unborn, and lectured me into the dark so effectively, that I began referring to him, in the privacy of my mind, as the Angel of Sleep.

The only thing that could keep me from drifting off was the occasional picture of a grotesquely misshapen newborn. The Angel of Sleep liked to include stark color photographs of specimen fetuses, horror-show blood-slick semi-human misfires, laid on a blue towel and set beside a ruler.

One had the face of a clown, the lips really that red and that big. Another had come out part fish, while a third had turned to stone. This one lacked a forehead, flat from the level of the eyebrows back. The eyes of that one were serenely hooded, like a swami's in samadhi. The pictures were often old Polaroids with a distinctly 1970s graininess. That only made sense, I remember thinking, since nowadays these kinds of defects would be caught early by ultrasound and aborted.

I imagined what it must have been like for women in antiquity to give birth to such conceptions. Stillbirths must have been the originals of gilled mermaids, trolls, and dwarfs. Grendel and Polyphemus—not to mention Ravana with his nine supernumerary heads—all must have forced their way into the human imagination through the human womb. *The human body*, I remember thinking, *is the mother of myth*. I also remember thinking, *I need to write that down*, and then something else about the sleep of reason, right before I fell asleep.

*

Or almost asleep. Conference-room sleep was such terrible sleep it scarcely qualified. It was, rather, a constantly disturbed twilight state, interrupted by polite subordinates' laughter at a joke, or the clearing of a throat, or a pager going off. Sometimes my eyes stayed blankly open, like a horse's, and I watched the text slides without reading them. I reverted to a purer, animal observation of light and shapes. The lecturer's words didn't correspond to meanings.

Somewhere in that parade of images and conditions and syndromes, I must have seen it. There would have been more than one Tuesday devoted to congenital heart defects. Yet I treated those lectures no differently than the ones on spina bifida or gastroschisis. No shiver of foreboding made me sit up straight and listen; no instinct pricked me to pay attention. Images of what you would be born with three years later flashed as big as the wall right there in front of me, and my eyelids did not flutter.

I suppose this failure to go pale with premonition has been true of every disease that will harm or kill the people I love. I have memorized facts about them, out of ambition or fascination, in a state of boredom or pre-exam jitters—never sensing my future intimacy with the beast.

It gets very, very easy to learn every last detail about a disease once someone you love gets diagnosed with it. The complex relationship of anatomy and physiology in heart defects used to make my eyes glaze over as a medical student. Within a day of your *in utero* diagnosis, I was scanning research articles on CHD as swiftly as newspaper articles, desperate for new, breaking details this source might have that the others didn't.

During morning conference, years before I became a father, I thought what I always did about congenital heart defects: that here was a tremendously complicated topic that would account, at most, for a single question on any given exam. I could skip the whole topic and spend the time I saved studying other topics, like the stories of Borges. I would simply guess "A" on the congenital-heart-disease question and still come out with a passing score.

I would memorize what I needed to know about the fetal heart, I assured myself, eventually, someday far in the future—which was as good, in that deliciously darkened conference room, as never.

If you notice, any time two castaways in a movie lay back, put their hands behind their heads and reflect how good it was to have survived the shipwreck, that's exactly when a gigantic shark smashes vertically through the raft. Or if six blandly attractive actors in their late teens show up at a secluded summer house on the shore of a secluded pond, and they unpack and explore the furnished rooms and gather to watch the sunset with a friends-forever air, you *know* that by sunup at least four will have been slaughtered by an axe murderer.

Anyway, I did the one thing you are never supposed to do at the beginning of a movie or novel (or memoir). A few days after your mother and I found out we were having twins, I sat back, set down my dictation microphone, and, more or less directly inviting fate to strike our growing family, I pondered the ways life had turned out great. I'd shaved two years off college and landed a radiology residency; the wife of my dreams (literally: see above) had landed the job of her dreams; in my spare time, I had taught myself to write; and now, to make things even better, I was getting *twins*. Twins! The most mystically cute form of offspring possible, and *exactly* the right number of offspring to allow you to *enjoy* their mystical cuteness, since triplets were obviously one too many, and quadruplets must turn the house into an apocalyptic daycare.

I floated into noon conference with the same secret joy. At one point, as our lecturer went on about the incidence of pancreatic mucinous cystadenocarcinoma, I actually shook my head in grinning disbelief at how lucky we were. Were we charmed? Was the world winnable? Was this really "life," which books kept claiming was full of woe and metastases and people beating the ground with their fists? Was the Buddha overstating human misery, or did your mother and I bat karmic home runs in our past lives?

Twins, I thought. This is going to be *great*.

Listen. In spite of everything that went down after you were born, and anything that is still to go down in the future, *I was absolutely right*. In fact, I never saw our lives as accurately as I did that afternoon, before the fetal heart survey.

Life *is* good.

We *are* charmed.

This *is* great.

Now let me tell you how you were diagnosed.

Ultrasound

A

There's only one real beauty secret:
symmetry.
In all the studies,
babies smile more at faces identical
to either side of the midline.

All you have to do to order
chaos
is duplicate it.
From the inkblot emerges a butterfly,
and from the scatter plot, a scatter pattern.

B

Eyes are twins, starstruck by evening's secret
symmetries.
Best is the studied
chaos a mirror reveals as order's identical
twin—sidereal, realigned.

Choice is chancy. The heart borders
on chaos,
duplicitous
even, especially, in love. Our desires fly
like gnats at nightfall, escaping pattern.

WE WAITED IN A DARK ROOM shortly after the positive pregnancy test. All it had given us was a plus sign. This would be the first time we saw anything.

Your mother reclined on the exam table, a clear jelly smeared over her bare, still-flat stomach. I held her hand while the ultrasonographer set the probe a few inches below your mother's navel and looked.

I kept my eyes on the monitor. I knew what a normal fetus looked like, and I also knew the alternatives, all too many of them. Fetus outside the uterus. Fetus that was once a fetus but had since dissolved, leaving a bubble stuck to the uterine wall. Fetus with no heartbeat. Fetus implanted too low, near the cervix, too close to the threshold of the world.

Your mother wasn't just watching the screen. She was also watching my face, using me as a rough indicator of good news or bad news. The face of her radiology-resident husband had clouded over with apprehension.

The ultrasonographer, still getting her bearings, had swept past what might, no, what *must* have been a fetus, but then, during the same sweep of the probe, another cluster of silver echoes flashed across the screen. This is what puzzled me, troubled me. Any anatomic area, sliced obliquely, is hard to recognize. That's why anatomy atlases always show a cross-section that's cut vertically or horizontally, but never, say, at 41 degrees slant. Slice a body slant, and you can't make head or tail, skull or coccyx of what you're seeing. This is even truer of fetal anatomy. I thought I had seen a single, disorganized, lumpen mass. I glanced at the ultrasonographer, looking for a rough indication of good news or bad news. Her face was expressionless. My mind raced, wondering if this were a molar pregnancy or some kind of hormone-secreting adnexal—

"They're twins," said the ultrasonographer.

Your mother and I looked at each other. Our faces broke into grins, and she gave a one-note laugh of joy and disbelief at our mad overwhelming luck. We'd bought one lottery ticket but hit two jackpots. I squeezed her hand.

"Here's one," said the ultrasonographer, pausing on a recognizably fetal image. What had I been worrying about? "And here's the other."

She paused and took a screen shot of this fetus. Pulling out a tray with a computer keyboard, she typed the label that appeared in the upper left corner of the screen.

TWIN   A

*

White and silver sparkles, dusting a black background: That's how we see our children for the first time.

To get the second ultrasound, at twelve weeks, we went to a different building and reported to Maternal-Fetal Medicine. MFM was where complex cases were handled by specialist obstetricians and ultrasound technologists. A twin pregnancy automatically qualified.

This time, the ultrasonographer took an unexpectedly long time and finally admitted she couldn't quite see the pulmonary artery on one of the twins. Would we mind too terribly much if she called in the doctor to take a look?

For a long while, your mother and I were left alone. "So what does this mean?" she asked me, gazing at a freeze-frame on the monitor.

"Probably nothing. They're trying to pick out super-tiny structures here. It's normal to have trouble seeing things."

"Could it be something bad?"

"Twins do have a higher incidence."

"Of?"

"Of everything." The fact came out before I had a chance to take the foreboding out of my tone of voice. "I mean, that's why we're here and not downstairs," I added quickly. "As for this—it's probably just a technical problem. Just because they can't *see* it doesn't mean it's not *there*. Happens all the time."

We waited in silence for several minutes more until the door finally opened. There stood the Angel of Sleep. He seemed to recognize me, but he didn't know me well enough for small talk. After a few words to introduce himself, he set about scanning, half his face ghost-white by screen light, the other half in darkness.

While he's scanning—and he's going to take his time before deciding what to tell us—I am going to tell you about ultrasound. You've had more ultrasound studies than any other kind. In the skilled hands of the Angel of Sleep, an ultrasound probe is about to make the critical diagnosis of your not-yet-started life. A few years later, ultrasound will miss something critical, and physics will play into it. I'll tell you about that, too, when the time comes.

When you do an ultrasound on an unborn child, you're basically swinging a flashlight made of sound. You swing it back and forth until you light on something familiar: An arm and hand, the fluorescent white line of a leg bone, a startlingly human profile. The structure you recognize serves as a landmark. As soon as you know where you are, you can start exploring. The head is north, the feet are south, the umbilical cord is in the middle.

Sounds easy enough, right? Only the fetus, if he or she is alive, is moving. The mother is breathing. Depending on how far along she is, the probe may be scanning a high, taut dome smeared with transparent jelly. Inevitably, the sonic searchlight slips. Tiny shifts of the hand can leave the probe staring into a night sea of amniotic fluid. Abnormalities are measured—and missed—by millimeters. That's why it takes years of practice, and a steady hand, to get any good.

We learned to see this way from bats. A bat sends out sound waves at a steady frequency and waits for the echoes. The echoes take an infinitesimally shorter or longer time to bounce back to the bat, depending on how close or far the stalactites and cave walls are. The ultrasound probe does the same thing, in principle. The water that cushions and nourishes a fetus will let sound waves right through. That's why amniotic fluid shows up onscreen as black. Eventually, the ultrasound waves hit the hard nibs and filaments of a fetal skeleton or the glowing raisin of a fetal brain. A fetus is alive and stubbornly solid. Its miniature body parts produce patterns of echoes. A computer algorithm converts those sound patterns into patterns of light, and the eye can recognize an image. Some fetal parts have more water in them, while others are bone-hard. The spectrum of echoes corresponds to a spectrum of light, from faint gray to magnesium-flare white.

The resolution is astonishing. At five weeks, ultrasound can pick up, at the center of a fetus, the steady winking of a bean inside the bean: the fetal heart.

And that is what the ultrasound saw inside your mother that afternoon. Two brothers, identical—except for their beating hearts.

A

Asymmetry's beautiful, too.
Who'd shlep all the way to Norway to

see the Northern Lights if all they did
was blink in a grid?

It's the crooked smile that disarms,
projects sincerity and charm.

Perfectly symmetrical faces belong in fashion ads and kitsch.
That's a less than human prettiness.

Asymmetry hints at a maker making on a scale so large the "flaws"
are features of a landscape. Pyramids impress. Himalayas awe.

Identical! Identical save for the heart, the heart.
This, too, is art.

I see, in asymmetry,
sublimity: the rightness of seas,

mismatched couplets, fingerprints;
of continents, pianos, planets, twins.

B

Symmetry comes from *with* and *measure*. Measure verse with verse
in a couplet, sleeve with sleeve on a shirt, but setting soul beside soul
compares the peerless with the peerless. Why should twins in the
same mother inherit the same luck in the same measure? Loneliness
alone my twins would have equally none of, a club with two members,
a gang of two not to be messed with. It's not the maker's way to make
one fate and double it. Life stories aren't written in heroic couplets.
Let their lives rhyme slant off their poet's hand. Asymmetry, I tell
myself, is not what sets the two of them apart; it is a part of the one
art they are. Twins. Identical! Identical save for the heart, the heart.

The obstetrician told us, at last, that he, too, could not see a pulmonary artery
on Twin A.

"This could be Tetralogy of Fallot," he said, looking at me, "with a very tight
stenosis. Otherwise it could be more serious, and the artery could be atretic."

This sounds like gobbledygook, I know. It sounded like that to your mother, too. The obstetrician was speaking physician to physician (unless he spoke
to patients that way), but he didn't realize it was gobbledygook to me, too. I had
memorized some stuff about Tet in medical school, but none of it came to mind
just then. My ears were not exactly hearing.

"My recommendation is for a repeat scan in three weeks to see if we can
get a better look at the anatomy. We will put you in contact with our genetic

counselor as well. After the next scan, depending on what we see or don't see, we may have to go on to a fetal echocardiogram."

I was all parent and no doctor. I translated, both for myself and your mother: "So, um, follow-up? You're saying, follow-up?"

He nodded, wondering, perhaps, if I was an idiot. (It was not the last time I would get this grimly disappointed look from him.) "Follow-up" could be a reassuring word in radiology parlance: It meant a finding was *concerning* without being *definite*.

"Yes," he said slowly. "A follow-up scan."

"Okay then, we'll come back for another scan. We'll follow up."

And so I grabbed that scrap of hope to share with your mother. We hurried home. With hindsight, I know that as early as that first ultrasound, his unforgiving gray eyes were far more certain of the diagnosis than we let ourselves think. I regarded the prospect of a problem with disbelief. If Twin B was clear, surely Twin A must have been doing a jig or something, turning and squirming during the scan? His spine must have gotten in the way of the acoustic searchlight, everything behind it thrown in shadow.

"I'll bet the next scan turns out normal," I promised your mother, sounding more confident than I felt. "They're just being overcautious, maybe because they know I'm a doctor or something. Don't worry. It's just a follow-up. I order these all the time."

We were living in a one-bedroom apartment then. It was right across the street from the hospital where I worked, the same hospital where you would be born. We asked the front office if we could break our lease and move to a larger apartment, but they told us they had nothing open.

We tried to rethink the two rooms we had to work with, mentally calculating occupants. Two babies; two parents; one, or at most two, grandparents to help out. How would we all fit? We guessed at ways to reposition the bed to accommodate two cribs. The geometry was stubborn. If we got rid of my desk, it just might work. To study or write, your mother explained, I could set the laptop on the kitchen table and, for silence, clap on my airport runway-issue, thirty-decibel Peltor earmuffs. We would make it work.

Unexpectedly, on the Thursday before Labor Day weekend, we got a call from the leasing office. A two-bedroom had opened up directly above us, but we would have to move into it immediately because the office had a second couple interested in our own apartment. We agreed, even though everyone who could have helped us move had left town that holiday weekend. I got on my lifting gloves and fetched a luggage cart from downstairs. Your mother, three months pregnant but looking six months along, started boxing up our things. All on one Saturday, waddling indefatigably, she did more than her part moving us out. I tried to get her to take breaks, but she went about the day's tasks with the patient diligence of a nesting mother bird. She was there to guide the box spring onto its side, there to slide it into the freight elevator. Sometimes she even took hold of our piled-high luggage cart and showed up in the doorway of the new apartment.

Your mother was buzzingly happy the whole time. "This was meant to be," she assured me. "This has all been arranged."

For the first time, I wondered whether she might have some preternatural ability to sway fate purely by prayer, closed off to the likes of cynical me. She had prayed hard for a bigger apartment, and something had opened up.

As we approached the date of the follow-up ultrasound, I realized the problem might be real. A little research had stripped my rationale for hope: many congenital heart defects were "sporadic"—which meant they could hit one identical twin but not the other. I found case reports that described problems in only one twin. Apparently, this kind of thing happened, and far more often than I had realized.

I kept returning to the way we had ended up in our two-bedroom apartment earlier that month. Could your mother's prayers work a similar wonder with your heart and pulmonary artery? "I know we couldn't see an opening last time," I imagined the ultrasonographer saying, her words identical to those of the leasing office. "But we have good news for you. Something has opened up."

Numerology, Embryology

ONE IS A SACRED NUMBER because all the Gods and Goddesses of the pantheon are really one. Two is a sacred number, too, because twins are how nature grants twice as much as two parents hoped for. But three is just as sacred, whether it's the *Tridev* of the Creator, Sustainer, and Destroyer in Hinduism, or the Holy Trinity of Christianity, or the three worlds of heaven, earth, and hell. The heart has four chambers; Islam's pillars are five. If three had a twin, they would together make six, the day of creation on which the ancient Hebrews believed human beings were created. Lucky number seven is that enigmatic miracle, a prime. Eight is for the Buddha's eightfold path. Nine is three times three, mystery multiplied by sacred mystery. Ten, by the grace of the Hindu zero, is sacred to secular knowledge since the whole world uses base ten mathematics. Physics could have gotten only so far with those ungainly Roman numerals; the zero was the wheel that set math and science rolling. Might every number be holy and mysterious at heart? Numbers measure every treasure. In the old days, *numbers* were another name for verse, for poetry.

Even numbers you wouldn't think are special are special. Twenty-three chromosomes in an ovum, twenty-three in a sperm cell.

> Meiosis, O my Muses: sing the separation
> of chromosomes, the Color Bodies
> that body forth the bodies that we are.
> Metaphase, anaphase, telophase:
> Meiosis, my oases, Muses, sing my sons
> blowing bubbles from a soap-dipped wand,
> listening worlds that lift and drift to the lawn,
> one bubble with a membrane through its heart,
> unless those are two bubbles, twinned,

conjoined at the skin, the only ones
too buoyant to brush the blades, two boys
shining, defiant, rising on the wind.

Put them together, and they make one fertilized egg, which begins to divide.
Mitosis: One becomes two, becomes four, becomes sixteen, becomes thirty-two.
Early on, if that microscopic pomegranate splits in half, each half becomes a
human being in full, with forty-six chromosomes. One becomes two.

Focus with me on three for a moment. In more than one tradition, there
are three worlds: the world above, the underworld, and this world between
them, where we live. Two are limitless, more or less, mysterious and unvisited,
higher and lower. The whole picture parallels what people saw when they first
stood on a shore: the sea that went down into the unknown, the sky that went
up into the unknown, and this scrim of habitable ground between. These, in
turn, corresponded to the eternity before birth, the eternity after death, and this
scrim of habitable time between.

How You Grew Your Heart

THREE WEEKS AFTER YOU WERE conceived, you existed in three layers: endoderm, mesoderm, and ectoderm. Your cells started out as cells that could become anything. Where they sorted out—into which of the three layers—determined their fates, their forms, their functions.

The endoderm, the inner layer, went on to become your "innards," your intestines, your liver, your pancreas. The ectoderm or outer layer went on to become your interface with the outside world. It's more than just the outer layer of skin and the enamel of your teeth. The brain finds out about its environment using retinas that see light, nerves that feel heat and pain, and an olfactory bulb that smells danger. So your sensors, your wiring, and your processor are all of a piece.

The ectoderm didn't start the process that led to your brain, however, until your middle layer, the mesoderm, signaled it should do so. Mesoderm is what gave rise to your heart.

Your heart is origami,
and on that paper is your secret name.

It started out creased a little skew,
like a love letter tucked inside
your chest in haste,

so they opened you
and folded you a little boat
whose every side was starboard.

When the boat sprang a leak,

they opened you again
and folded you a little crane
who beat her wings and beat and beat her wings

until she was beat, so beat

they opened you a third time
and folded you a living flame
that draws to this day light and heat

from those words of love
discovered in your treasure chest,
the rhythm in you that begins you with

> *Your heart is origami,*
> *and on the paper is your secret name.*

Whatever the body system, the embryo makes a hollow where there wasn't one before. Simply form a tube, and life will make something flow through it— air, blood, lymph, bile, or an electrical impulse. Blocked flow through a tube describes a whole slew of common diseases: heart attack, stroke, jaundice, clots in the leg veins, pulmonary embolism, and bowel obstruction. When all the flowing stops through all the tubes, that's death.

Your three embryonic layers, when they got the signal to form their specific tissues, started curling into tubes and twisting. This held true even for parts of your body you wouldn't think of as being particularly tubular. The skin is a sack full of organs and bones, and those bones, in turn, are hollow—stronger that way than if they were solid bars. The lungs have their bronchial windpipes, and the brain has its ventricles. "Ventricle" is Latin for *belly* or *stomach*, the organ which gives us our first and most intense experience of our own hollowness. Even the spinal cord, in cross-section, has a tiny perforation at its center. "Solid" organs like the liver and spleen are actually shot through with tiny ducts.

The cells you are made of, seen under a microscope, turn out to be sacks full of cellular equipment: the mitochondria (itself a sack), the Golgi apparatus (which is made up of *cisternae*, Latin for "boxes"), vesicles (Latin for "bladders"), and the nucleus. The nucleus is supposedly the cell's "kernel," but it's really just a sack full of DNA.

You are hollows within hollows within hollows—at their center, the four-chambered hollow at, or rather *of*, your heart. The heart twists into its form like a balloon-puppet. A layer folds into a tube, and the tube twists, divides itself, and links up with other tubes. You can see the signs of those twists in the way a heart is cocked to one side and in the way the major arteries swoop around a little as they leave the heart. The arch of the aorta isn't in line with the breast-bone; it starts out slightly to the right of midline, then swings left as it rises. The heart divides itself with a little nub of tissue that flattens into partitions between the right and left chambers.

These tubes and inner walls twisted, aligned, and fused very early in your body's development. You were still a fetus, bean-shaped and bean-sized. Development isn't a game of inches; it's a game of micrometers.

At some point in your development, there was a micrometer's offset in those fusing, twisting tubes. As you got bigger, so did the offset.

Your heart was off by a mini-smidgen at Week Five. Nine months later, when you had quintupled your weight, you had a gaping hole in the wall between your heart's chambers, a missing segment of pipe, and a size mismatch between your heart's nozzle and your aorta's hose.

On your next ultrasound, the doctor gave us a tour. He showed us each problem, one by one. The diagnosis was confirmed, and it was a mouthful: "Pulmonary Atresia with Ventricular Septal Defect."

He sat us down and gave us the talk.

In a human chest, a bunch of tubes crisscross, loop, and crowd a small space, and they are all crucial to human life. The inside of your ribcage can get downright messy. Consider how the heart and great vessels look in *Gray's Anatomy*. Ignore those dozen or so tubes at the top of the picture. Focus on the black box at the center. That rectangle-ish bullet hole through the center: I colored that in. That's what you were born without. That missing bit of tube caused everything. It seems outrageous that your life should depend on so small an absence. If it seems small in the picture, think about this: prenatally, when the problem occurred, that spot was a thing of millimeters.

You'll notice at the top of the black box those two branches, a left and a right. In an embryo, these two branches form separately, meet in the middle, and hook up to the trunk (the part you were born without). It's not like a tree where the trunk gives rise to the branches. So you did have those two branches—but without the trunk, nothing connected them to the heart.

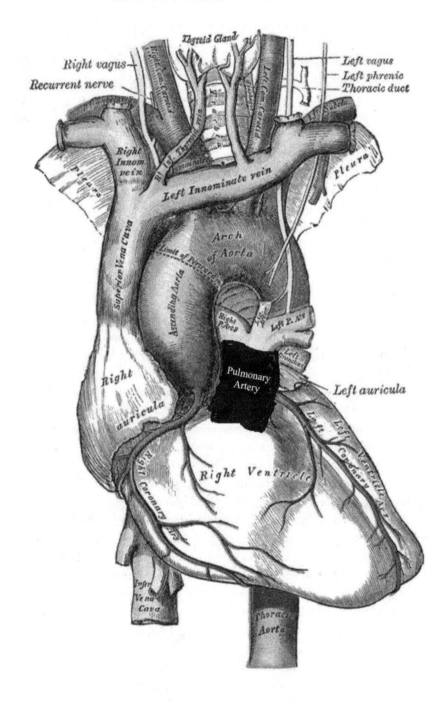

The other part of your defect involved something inside the heart, the wall between the two ventricles (the left one pumps blood to your body, the right one pumps blood to your lungs). The top part of that divider didn't form, either, but you can't see it in this picture because it's inside the heart. Again, though: millimeters!

Immediately after you were born, a natural connection from the big curved tube (the aorta) to your pulmonary artery branches kept you alive. Blood from the aortic arch poured down into your two pulmonary artery branches and out to your lungs to get oxygenated. After birth, that connection, the ductus, seals up naturally. As soon as you were taken out of your mother, the doctors hooked you up to an IV drug that kept the ductus open.

So the plumbing is complicated, but the concept isn't. We are made of tubes, and we have to flow to stay alive.

The heart connects to the lungs through the T-shaped pulmonary artery. In the lungs, the blood picks up oxygen from the air you breathe. That oxygenated blood comes back to the heart and gets pumped out to the body through the aorta and its arteries. After giving up its oxygen where the body needs it, the blood comes back to the heart. This deoxygenated blood gets pumped to the lungs again. That's the cycle. You were born missing a connection between your heart and your lungs—the bottom part of the T-shaped pulmonary artery. You also had an oversized aorta that didn't fit your heart's outlet. A heart is supposed to have a wall between its ventricles (to keep oxygenated and deoxygenated blood from mixing). That wall had a hole in it.

Another frustrated attempt at describing the problem. I want to come up with some other way for you to visualize this. I want it to be clear and straightforward and simple, but this material, as I can attest, is hard for medical students to grasp, even after late nights picking at a formalin-pickled body. My radiologist-self describes anatomy. My poet-self makes metaphors. I want those twin selves to collaborate on an image. Your red blood cells become blood red pomegranates, your blood vessels become one-way roads, your heart becomes a warehouse that collects the pomegranates and sends them out.

Imagine you're the biggest pomegranate supplier in the country. You have one giant warehouse that sends truckloads of pomegranates all over the country every hour on a giant one-way highway. That warehouse is your heart. The highway is your aorta, going out to your body.

Your warehouse sends trucks out to pick up those pomegranates. So those trucks leave for your two vast pomegranate orchards, one to the east, one to the west. Those two orchards are your left and right lungs.

A broad, one-way main road leaves the back of that distribution center. This main road ends in a T. Half your trucks take a left and reach the left orchard, and the other half go right to reach the right orchard. They're loaded up with pomegranates there. The broad, one-way main road is your main pulmonary artery. At the T, it splits into your left and right pulmonary arteries.

When you were still forming in the womb, some of the construction work went wrong.

First, the warehouse. You have to keep the trucks with pomegranates in them apart from the trucks that are empty, so empty trucks don't accidentally go out to the highway, and full trucks don't go out to the orchards. The wall between empty trucks and full trucks never got finished. So some trucks end up on the wrong side of the warehouse.

The major problem, though, is the main road going from the warehouse to the orchards. It never got paved. The construction workers paved the top crossbar of the T, but not its bottom part. Sometimes they have been known to scrimp and make that main road too narrow—but in your case, they just forgot to make a road there at all.

What to do, what to do? The high-demand season is coming—birth—and you have to get your trucks out to your orchards. Keep this road map in your mind for later. I'll return to it when I explain your later surgeries.

Needles

22q11.2 DELETION SYNDROME causes mental retardation, psychiatric disorders, seizures, kidney anomalies, cleft palate, and AIDS-like immune system problems because the thymus fails to develop.

Alagille syndrome causes liver damage from crooked, narrow bile ducts. Pebbles of solid cholesterol lodge under the skin. Instead of box-shaped vertebral bodies, your spine is made of bone butterflies.

Patau syndrome, or Trisomy 13, causes "abnormal genitalia," which could mean anything, none of it good. Ditto "intellectual disability" and "motor disorders." Cyclopia is what Polyphemus in the *Odyssey* had. Blindness can be due to defects involving any part of the eye, from the iris to the retina.

Shortly after the diagnosis, we met with a "genetic counselor," who showed us some glossy pamphlets about the various kinds of sequencing techniques.

I remember staring at the little fluorescent green chromosomes all in a row. They had the look of little Norse runes. The rune a human chromosome looks the most like is X, *gebo*. The meaning of that rune is "gift."

Getting the amniocentesis was the "right" thing to do. I knew what the Angel was telling me was true. "It is a safe procedure in the right hands," he insisted. "Not without risk, but safe, and we really must get all the information so that we can advise you."

Ah, those neutral word choices! I had used them myself when calming people about the needles I was going to stick into their organs. "More information" meant that he had to clear Chromosome 22, the most likely abnormal one. "Not without risk, but safe" meant that a 7.5 cm hollow harpoon of a needle would gore your mother's baby bump, but the last however-many-we've-done-up-here went fine, so relax. "Advise you" meant advise us to abort.

"I think we're okay," I said awkwardly.

Maybe this was not the customary way the procedure was declined, if it was declined at all by physician-parents. He paused and stared at me. "You had the discussion with the genetic counselor?"

"Yes."

"So you understand it is, medically speaking, very important? Critical?"

It was strange to hear that usually tired-sounding voice take on a note of frustration. He was staring at me as he spoke because he knew I was a fellow physician—surely I could be counted on to convince my wife to do the right thing? The words were reasonable, but the tone said, *You're a doc, and you're refusing the amnio? Are you kidding me?* My mind, at the cue of his voice, switched into its Tuesday-morning-conference state, half samadhi, half catatonia. I had no anxiety.

Some questions I should have asked: If the amnio comes back showing a genetic problem, does it mean that both brothers have it?

With the brothers sharing a placenta, does aborting one brother risk aborting the other, too?

Is it ethical, or fair, or anything but atrocious to pick Twin B to live, and Twin A not to, just because Twin A doesn't match nature's default "Normal" setting?

Your mother and I never asked these questions of him, or of ourselves. The best way we had to avoid these questions was by refusing to ask the *first* question: The question that took the form of a needle. We didn't have some drawn-out, late-night, soul-searching discussion on the ramifications of an amniocentesis. We had glanced at each other the instant he brought it up. That's how long it took us to decide. Even the visit with the genetic counselor had been a formality, more for their sake than ours.

"I think we'll pass," I said lightly, as if I were refusing dessert.

His face went pink. He murmured something and got out of the room, presumably to cool off. I didn't feel anything. Your mother and I looked at each other. I shrugged.

I want you to know that he wasn't seeking some personal or professional gratification by advocating the amnio (and, depending on what its results were, abortion). This doctor had seen what kinds of lives children with genetic syndromes were condemned, by parental squeamishness or parental ideology, to live. He wanted to slide that amnio needle into your mother's belly—within centimeters of you and your unborn brother—*out of mercy.*

It was already too late. If he had wanted us to get the amnio, he should have known better than to show us your faces. We already loved you.

*

I knew what the needle actually *looked* like—a 90 mm, 22-gauge stainless steel
needle with beveled tip and sideport. It's not a forgettable image. Going through
some old Word files, I found the ode I wrote to that haunting needle. I even
slipped your future name into it ("shiv" in English is a stabbing weapon), though
I don't know if we had chosen your name yet. As you can see, the ode to the
needle took on the shape of the needle.

> Amnio
> needle,
> coolly
> doing
> the needful,
> you
> long &
> godless
> straw
> sipping
> only
> the holiest
> of waters,
> mosquito
> proboscis
> siphoning
> off
> the sole
> repast
> richer
> than
> a blood
> meal,
> sterile
> stainless
> steel
> investigating
> flawed &
> fertile

flesh,
crossing
borders,
lost
to awe,
serpent
fang
piercing
eternity
to introduce
the venom
of your
question,
the world's
smallest
sniper
scope
hunting
the world's
biggest
hope,
push pin
popping
the mystery,
vandal
slashing
vulnerably
ancient
airlocked
art,
deft
shiv
angling
to stab
more
than one
body
straight

through
the
heart.

If one of us had pushed for the amnio, the other would have almost certainly acquiesced, misgivings and all. Still, the last checkpoint was your mom.
The body put to the question was hers; the final decision was hers, whether to
let that cold nonhuman steel into her body or not. The equal claim of your heart
to beat was never in doubt on our end. We wanted you any way that chance or
karma gave you to us. And not once, in spite of everything that happened after,
did we regret that afternoon's decision.

Repeating the Echo

FROM THERE ON OUT, we had to make appointments with the pediatric cardiologists. They would be the ones scanning you from now on, with special attention to your heart. They called the study a fetal echocardiogram, a fancy name for an ultrasound. You and your brother got a bunch of these studies at regular intervals before you were born. The first confirmed the diagnosis you'd already gotten. The second—the interestingly named "repeat echo"—added a little havoc to the mayhem.

We had never met this particular cardiologist before. She happened to be assigned to read fetal echoes the day we were scheduled. She was pink-cheeked and bespectacled, and everything she said had a chipper lilt to it. Her tone and manner were so upbeat that even when she took out pen and paper and began to draw a diagram, we couldn't quite process that she was voicing an even-worse doom on you.

"So, what they've been saying is, 'Oh, it's pulmonic atresia, it's pulmonic atresia!' But based on what *I'm* seeing, I think this is actually a *truncus!*"

Italics and exclamation points may seem out of place, but believe me, they only hint at the confusing indirection of her tone of voice. As she spoke, she was drawing a *new* heart defect, one that gave rise to a giant vessel that swept to the top of the page. This mega-vessel covered both outlets of the heart. It wasn't that one artery needed to be tacked into place, and that the other one hadn't formed. They had both fused into a single, monstrous firehose.

"So naturally, this really, you know, changes things! It's a *lot* more surgically involved!"

I eyed her briskly working pen, her high eyebrows, her ruddy cheeks. These chipper verbal patterns, like your best friend's mom saying we'll all go out to ice cream after the game, were contradicted by her pen's keen, ruthless, swift movements. I could see through to the real brilliance she had learned to hide with her manner. A woman starting out back in the 1980s, in a rarefied subspecialty of pediatrics—this voice must have kept the Good Old Boys from feeling threatened. By now, it must have become second nature. Even her bad-news tone had no sharp edges.

And brilliant she was: We were sitting across from her, but she didn't have to spin the paper to show us. She was drawing this complex diagram of fetal circulation *upside down*. I read her nametag, the full title under her name. She was head of the department, the expert, the final word.

Your mother and I walked out of the hospital hand in hand into a very sunny day. The worst news came to us, consistently, under incongruous sunshine. This latest doctor's voice had sunshine in it, too.

We looked around us: Case University students with backpacks and iPods walking along Euclid Avenue, buses with smiling malpractice lawyers on the side, hospital-entrance begonias, a van parked with its wheelchair platform descending. The details baffled me. Where had all these noisy sparrows come from? How could the sky and city be so happy and hyperactive?

We had decided, before this echo, to get pizza afterward from a place on campus called Rascal House Pizza. Automatically, hand in hand, we piloted one another to the programmed destination. Neither of us seemed to lead. Our ritual was to order a medium with pineapple, hurry it to the table hot from the oven, and eat each steaming piece very gingerly. We did everything as usual, as if defying this new development to ruin our lunch date. We said nothing while we waited. Automatically, without blowing on the pieces, we ate. Nothing had any taste. No texture, either, save for the rough-slick spot where I burned the roof of my mouth. My tongue worried it for the rest of the day.

The very next fetal echo, a few harrowing weeks later, downgraded your diagnosis from truncus arteriosus back to PA-VSD. We had thought PA-VSD was the worst-case scenario, but it wasn't even close to the top of the worst-case-scenario hierarchy. (On the very tippy-top of which, I guess, is death.) Once, we had sobbed that you had PA-VSD, this complex malformation. Now we hugged each other and gave thanks to the Gods that this was all you had.

And we had every reason to do so. Because the world—and the waiting room, and the neonatal ICU—was full of fetuses and newborns worse off than you.

> Who is the weathervane
> to question the will of the wind?

This little baby had water balloons where her kidneys should have been. This little baby was born with his intestines spilling out, as if he'd gotten in a knife fight with God. This little baby had chalk for bones, and this little baby had molasses for mucus. And this little baby had jelly instead of muscle, and I went to elementary school with him, and at the first funeral I ever attended, he was there. We used to call dibs on who got to push his wheelchair. This little baby had a wound-red cleft in the small of her back. This little baby, his spine a spiral staircase, mysteriously injured in the brain, was wheeled from specialist to specialist for thirty-six years, and in all those years, he never spoke a word, and never kissed a girl, and never read a book. He died of pneumonia in a hospital, and I used to play *Contra* with his little brother, and once I helped tilt him so his mother could dab his bedsore.

It was possible, after that blessed false alarm, to rethink self-pity and quit our baseline gnashing-of-teeth, to think and even to say aloud, *Ami, how lucky we are, Ami, he's getting off easy.*

The Parting of the Hair

2007 WAS A YEAR OUR family burgeoned. Imagine expecting twin sons while your sister is expecting her second child—at the same time! Your mother, having twins, had a baby bump that kept pace with your aunt's, four months further along. Your aunt Shilpa took care of HIV patients full-time in the Cook County health system until the day before her delivery. The date of our baby shower timed out two weeks after your aunt's Caesarian section—but she bundled an infant Keya in the car and drove the six hours to be there with us, and in a *saree* at that. The women in our family have always been energetically superhuman. Your immigrant grandmother, at an identical age back in the early 1980s, studied for her medical board exams while stirring a pot of dahl and bobbing baby Amit off to one side. A few volts of her energy, transmitted through the perch of her hip, have carried me forty years.

During the third trimester, we held a ceremony for your mother that is the equivalent of a baby shower. It's called the *simantonayan*, the Parting of the Hair. Three dozen of us in traditional dress packed the apartment building's second-floor common room, their lively pinks and blues contrasting with the drab grays of the one working elevator. Your grandfather chanted Sanskrit hymns, and assembled relatives clapped and sang for you. Gifts for you and your twin brother collected in a ziggurat on one of the round tables. Sometimes I circled back to your newborn niece Keya, big-eyed and swaddled and calm. I felt no nervousness about welcoming two such babies in a few months. I did not imagine hospital rooms or intensive care units, either. No one we knew had been in this situation before, so our imaginations had no raw materials to pre-construct a future. That blessing let us enjoy the larger, twin blessing we celebrated that day.

Your aunt Shilpa shifted the part in your mother's hair from one side to the other. It was the page of a book being turned, and two new characters would be introduced in the chapter. At the end of the ceremony, your mother pressed her swollen feet on blue paint and made footprints on a long roll of white paper. Time that always passed, paused; she stepped into the same river twice, holding the folds and layers of her deep blue saree off the floor. I remembered how she used to twiddle her toes and admit, bashfully, *I'm terribly vain about my feet*—and how she stomped them fiercely during her classical Indian dances, thumping the stage, the opposite of airy ballet; I remembered the large red circle painted on the tops of her feet on our wedding day; remembered her painting her nails on the bathroom floor while watching *Friends* on the laptop. Time that had paused, passed. The steps on the white paper were all forward, into our new life. I followed them in my mind, like pasted steps on a studio floor.

In the corner, consecrating that room as he would a dance stage, pulsed a bronze sculpture of the cosmic dancer Shiva Nataraja. He is your namesake. He awakens and dances the dance of destruction in a sphere of fire at the end of time. Under his foot is a dwarf named Apasmara, Amnesia. It takes a catastrophe, a cosmic fireball, to end one phase of existence and inaugurate the next. Out of that devastation: wisdom. The foregone amniocentesis, the heart defect, the possibility of graver problems—these things were completely out of everyone's mind, though a few family members there knew about them. Always remember, Shiv, that none of that prenatal doomsaying smudged the celebration. We welcomed your two souls without reservation, without apprehension. Outside, anemic autumn sunlight spread thinly over the bricks and potholes of downtown Cleveland. We welcomed the future that would come to us that winter. The ceremony gave that day the thrill and swell of early spring.

Deliverance

IT'S AN INTERESTING VERB, *to deliver*. People use it most often for packages delivered to the porch. In the old cartoons of my childhood, storks delivered newborn babies. That image came from a fable by Hans Christian Andersen—in Northern Europe, storks migrate south for nine months, the typical length of a pregnancy.

If someone *delivers*, it means that he or she comes through when it counts. You can also *deliver a blow*, that is, hit someone, hurt someone—but you can also deliver someone *from* something, liberating that person from suffering or danger.

While your lungs sucked in and squeezed out amniotic fluid, you were fine. Your arteries circulated the umbilical cord blood your mother sent you from her lungs. It's only once you were *delivered* that the trouble started. The obstetrician who delivered your mother delivered you into the mortal danger it would take all of modern medicine to deliver you from.

Heart leads, monitor wires, IV pole: You are lost in the jungle. It isn't right to say you've been abandoned, but no one is holding you, and your back and head are flat on the bassinet. It's cushioned, but that surface is a stone cot compared to what you're used to.

Picking you up has not been officially authorized. *Not* picking you up has not been officially forbidden. Your idiot father cannot tell the difference. He stands beside your bassinet, sticking his finger in your palm. It's like being thrown a rescue ring at sea and grabbing it, but the rope stays slack. The rescuer behind the high rail just stares at you, for some reason not pulling you out of that frigid North Sea.

There is some uncertainty about how soon you will have to go to your first surgery. This will be a stopgap repair, a shunt to let oxygen-rich blood get to the body that needs it. Later, when your soul has thrown down some deeper roots in your physical being, you will be cracked open and remade.

On that first day, given the uncertainty, you could not drink milk because "they" might "take" you at any moment. This meant you might have to be put under anesthesia emergently, and you can't go under with food in your stomach—the milk might surge back up your esophagus and pour down your unprotected windpipe, filling your lungs. The blue mini-bottle of Pedialyte is no substitute. Your mother's breastmilk is the good stuff: whey protein, serum albumin, sphingolipids, phospholipids, cytokines, lysozyme, creatine, creatinine, nucleotides, immunoglobulins from IgA to IgZ, amino acids, oligosaccharides, erythropoietin, alpha-1-antitrypsin—just hitting the highlights feels like I'm gargling a mouthful of Latin poetry.

Pedialyte, by contrast, is the basics: H_2O, sodium, potassium, chloride, dextrose. Water, sugar, salt. You hate it, and who would blame you?

I put on a sterile glove and let you root to my pinky, bare hand on the few exposed or accessible parts of you, feeding your skin the touch of skin. How long does it take me to ask? An hour? A day? I do not or cannot or will not remember. Finally, I stop a nurse who has just popped in and ask: "Can I hold him? Is that possible?"

It's not so casually accomplished, of course: Wires and tubes have to be safeguarded, and your body has to be set down gingerly on my lap because I am a new dad and too paranoid about dropping you to scoop you myself. I get into the chair and wait, raising my knees a little to keep you from sliding. At last, you touch down safely. It is awkward. I don't know where to put my elbows. The pillow, here to make me deceptively mother-soft, I suppose, feels dangerously round. I worry you're going to roll right off it.

The knit cap the nurse has put on you, rainbow crosshatch with a red ball on top, I still possess. I keep it in my study on the highest bookshelf, on top of the Gita, something like the mantle over a Torah. These NICU caps, I found out later, were knit by volunteers in local nursing homes, but there's no way of tracing who, specifically, knit yours. I keep it as a reminder of your first days. It is a reminder, also, of unseen hands, somewhere in the city, knitting.

2

HANDS

Twinned Poems

SOMETIMES, WHEN I WROTE a poem about you, the poem would twin itself. The second poem wasn't a rewrite of the first. The two poems were different poems in the same form.

Like these, which I wrote shortly after you and your brother were born. They're twinned poems about having twins. Naturally, I wrote both poems in couplets. Their form is an ancient Arabian form called a *ghazal*. Rhymes crowd the form because no art form delights in twos quite like poetry. Symmetry is beauty wearing its soul on the surface. That's why all you need to do to transform chaos into an eye-catching pattern is double it. If a word's sound is its genome, rhyming is twinning. Two different words make the same sound. You and your brother are different people made of the same genes. Twin A, Twin B: Poem A, Poem B.

A

She pushed and hissed and pushed. Our twin sons crowned like echoes
Of each other, off each other, bouncing baby echoes.

Depth is an illusion, words a murmuration of starlings
Whose surface, folding and unfolding, sounds its own echoes.

One twin rooted by reflex to the breathing tube taped to his cheek.
When they slid it out, his throat, grated raw, was a fountain of echoes.

His mother could not bear to sleep apart from him,
Either breast's milk-ache a burial mound of echoes.

TWIN A

Twin sons! I prayed their health might be symmetric, prayed
Death was an illusion, a mirage grounded in echoes.

All my life, I sought beauty through symmetry.
On becoming a father, I found it in echoes.

B

If a new life adds a new word, our love gave birth to rhymes.
We still give thanks for the tang of sour milk and earthy rhymes.

Twin A under anesthesia, Twin B in a bassinet,
Identically hushed. I'll take a decade finding worthy rhymes.

Baby monitor at home, telemetry in the Unit:
My divided memory shuttles back and forth for rhymes.

I snipped the blood braid and thought of Atropos,
The third inflexible Fate who orphans rhymes.

I risked two ghazals only after fatherhood
Gave my mother tongue this twinfinite source of rhymes.

Hands

YOUR HEART STOPPED a little after midnight on the third day.

If a heart lead gets dislodged, the alarms go off—but you hadn't moved in my lap. Meanwhile, the room monitors had gone crazy. It was like walking into a supermarket and you're their millionth customer, sirens and flashing lights, everything but the multicolored balloons falling from the ceiling. I glanced up at your heart monitor.

Flatline.

I should have panicked. I'm not certain why I didn't. My hand made the decision. It leapt off the armrest and flicked the left side of your chest, roughly where I knew the tip of your heart should be. An old-fashioned, desperate measure to resuscitate a heart is the "precordial thump," where you knock the chest with the butt of your fist. I think that was somewhere in my memory.

A few seconds later, the nurses had charged the room, but your heart was beating again, the luminous green line going bump, dip, spike, dip, bump. I explained what had happened. The nurse printed out a strip from the machine that showed the recent asystole, and the on-call resident studied it at the nurses' station, knee bobbing, biting his fingernails.

Hands.

Your mother and I had already met, a few weeks before your birth, with your pediatric cardiothoracic surgeon. He was an Egyptian, slight of build and mustached, and the hand I shook turned out to be smaller than I expected. I had assumed a Pediatric CT surgeon must have a violinist's fingers, longer than normal, maybe even double-jointed at the knuckles. Aspiring surgery fellows would be chosen or excluded on the basis of an inspection: *This one we'll train; he's got the Hands.* Dr. Hennein's handshake was dry and not particularly firm.

In his immense office, he sat at a table with us and showed us what he would do using a plastic model of the heart. My eyes kept flicking to the wall of monitors behind him, each one with a different child's vitals on it, linked in real time to his ICU beds. He was never not on call.

He took half of the heart off to show us the cross-section.

"So we take this overriding aorta and bring it in so it's over the left ventricle. We seal up the hole in the septum, which would be right here. Then we put in a conduit from the right ventricle out to the branch pulmonary arteries, which he has, because they develop separately from the main PA."

To hear him tell it, the whole surgery was as stressful as darning socks on the porch on Sunday. And for him, it probably was. His tone wasn't *casual*, although that's the word that comes to your mother's mind when she thinks about our conversation with him. I remember it differently, or rather I remember it in two different ways.

In one version, his voice has the unflappable quiet of total certainty about his skill. "This is what I am going to do": Not "I will *try* to do this," not "I *hope* to do this." He was so skilled, utterly in command of his instruments, that he made factual statements about the future. And no matter how softly he spoke, the future was listening up. The future would toe the line.

In my other memory, he was slightly bored. This was his standard PA-VSD discussion; just press Play. He was reciting the script live for our benefit. The rest of our interaction with CT surgery would go through his three warmhearted nurse practitioners, who saw us for the follow-up visits, handled the phone calls, and did the requisite hand-holding. He had no time for such things; he had his hands full. Maybe all three moods—offhand, self-confident, bored—coexisted during that conversation. What did it matter whether he was compassionate or detached? His role, he knew, came down to his hands. The more detached he stayed, the better, maybe: some higher-order tasks require the Zenlike no-mind of golfers and yogis. At that desk, he handled the heart—your heart, metaphorically—with total ease. He shelled it open and set everything straight. In the old days of medicine, surgeon = God. I became a believer.

Afterward, as the date approached, I kept thinking about his fingers. What if he slammed his fingers in a car door? What if, playing basketball with his kid, he got careless grabbing a rebound? Couldn't some device be designed for such hands? I wanted two temperature-controlled, lightweight safes that would seal around either wrist, protecting his hands during all the time he was outside the OR. Fingers struck me as part bug-antennae, part twigs, too bendy and brittle for a human life to depend on them. Though I suppose a radiologist's eyeballs are much the same: fragile, crucial, vulnerably doctoring the vulnerable.

It's those hands—mortal, human, fallible—that are waiting for you downstairs, in the OR.

You are on the move now. Do you know where you are going? Probably not. But you know you are moving. As the bassinet gets wheeled out of the room, the fluid in your inner ears begins to stir, riding the loop-de-loop of the semicircular canals. Inside them, fine crystals tickle into sensation, and your brain registers movement.

How much do you really know right now? When you're hungry, is it a purely physical pang, or do you also get that desperate feeling inside? When you experience pain at this age, as you will, inevitably, do you *feel* pain, or merely *sense* it?

A baby's brain looks unmistakable on a CT. The crinkles are not as deep, and the fine gradations of gray are missing. The brain hasn't fully sleeved its axons with myelin yet. Myelin, the "insulation" of neural wiring, is mostly fat. In the centuries before baby formula, the body made its myelin entirely from one source: mother's milk, carrying every thought and emotion.

So soon after birth, your brain is mostly a sack of water. It's an open question whether you are self-aware in the way we use that term. You don't know where you are. You can't conceptualize time yet. It will still be months before you even discover the body you inhabit, delighting in your head, shoulders, knees and toes, knees and toes.

Right now, even your hands have something independent about them. Your hands guide themselves relentlessly to your mouth (or would, if it weren't for the tubing). Your mouth, too, seeks out whatever brushes the skin near it, even when your eyes are ointment-sealed. Everything is automatic.

Which may be a mercy. Hunger is real, but worry is not yet possible, neurologically. Pain is real, but desperation is not yet possible, either.

Or are the hunger and pain worse than anyone else's? The perception of pain results, like so much else, from a balance of inhibition and disinhibition. Pain receptors shout from the periphery, and the mind can either mute or magnify their shout. It's why people have different pain tolerances. You have been *nil per os*, nothing by mouth, before surgery; after surgery, you will have five wire loops in your breastbone. Are your pain and hunger the purest pain and the purest hunger? The roads to your interior are all open. There are no checkpoints. You don't have anything to counteract your pain and hunger, no faith, no philosophical objectivity, no distractions. No *inhibitory descending pathways*, by which the brain persuades the body not to feel what it feels.

The more I think about your pain and hunger as a newborn, the less I can distinguish it from the pain of animals: absolute and unrelenting.

But for now, let's just say you're not scared or worried. And once the anesthesia kicks in, you're not even hungry anymore. Think of this as a temporary reprieve. Think of this black hole moment, eyelids taped shut and a tube down your throat to breathe for you, as the best you have felt since the minute you were born.

Outside the OR, while an assistant is smearing your chest with dark brown iodinated cleanser, your surgeon is scrubbing in. He lathers up and abrades his precious hands using a sterile rectangular brush, getting under the fingernails. A foot pedal lets him rinse his arms up to the elbows. He touches nothing on his way into the suite, hands held up and away, like two alligator clamps connected to a high-voltage battery. The size 7 ½ sterile gloves lie in Gideon Bible-delicate wrapping paper, and he unfolds them, first the midline crease, then the side flaps. On a nearby table: an assortment of fresh blades, a device for inflicting pinpoint electrical burns, a motorized baby buzzsaw.

He is ready for you.

It is time.

Dewdrop and Rosebush

ONCE UPON A TIME, Dewdrop was sad.

"I am not a raindrop. I didn't fall from heaven. I am not a teardrop. No one cried me. Every morning, I am born on this rose. Sometimes on a leaf, sometimes on a petal, sometimes on a thorn. Sometimes high up the stem and sometimes low. But by midday, I always burn away. By dawn, I do return—but not to stay."

Rosebush laughed. "Dewdrop, only part of you burns away. The other part of you I drink into myself. You water my flowering and grow my fragrance. These are as much yours as they are mine. On petal, leaf, or thorn, I wear you as a jewel. You come back in the morning because you are needed here. You leave at midday because the sky loves you."

Dewdrop rejoiced to learn this about herself. Now she welcomed the sunlight. Brighter and brighter, smaller and smaller, until she was all gone. No, not gone: She knew better now. She was one with the Rosebush and one with the heavens. Part of her answered the thirst of the roses. Part of her answered the call of the clouds.

As midday approached, she sang to Rosebush, "I would have rejoiced had I gotten to stay. But it's still a joy to depart and a joy to return the next day. A joy to be born and a joy to burn away. A joy to be here and a joy to go there. May I fold into fragrance and join the air."

I got to thinking, around this time, waiting infinitely in the pre-op holding area, about parenting. I thought how human beings possess an involuntary perpetuity that intersects with voluntary self-perpetuation. The involuntary part is birth (or rebirth, as we would have it). The voluntary part is parenting.

Your self is born and borne within you when, after many goings-hence, you come to be once more. You, newborn, emerged as an extension of your mother, her body split by the crowning head, connected at the navel. You emerged orthogonal to her lying-in, like a sapling risen from the supine nurse log. Death, there, is the substrate of life. Karmically, rebirth is the sole substrate of rebirth. Past lives mulch the karmic soil of your present one. You parented yourself, in that sense.

But you are two kinds of generational culmination: That of your blood-line and that of the strangers you have been in your past lives. Your biological ancestors and your karmic ones. Those two lineages intersect at the relationship between parent and child. I did not know the past people you were, but I met you at the start of your migration through this body to your next one. For now, I was given, I thought, the chance, the sacred duty, to direct you toward truth and beauty, or at least hold you a while before you went under the knife.

I like to imagine scenarios of lost loved ones reborn. In a poignant pregnant irony, mutually unaware, a great-grandson might do a kindness to a great-grandfather, disguised in the body of a stranger; and the great-grandfather would know nothing of his soul-sleeve three generations back, and the great-grandson would have no idea he just met and helped his own distant ancestor.

We are all of us mysteriously networked neurons. Love manifests in the species like a thought in the brain. Go far enough back, and who isn't family?

I don't want to return to the physical world, to the world of this story, where you are set to go into the OR and we are terrified to send you in but even more terrified not to.

It feels like a breather to write about something else for a bit. A bit of escapism from the fluorescent tube lights, your ID wristband, the Dixie cup full of forgetfulness the nurse delivered to you, a little preliminary sip of oblivion. The physical world is stubborn. It can't be shaped and reshaped, drafted and revised as easily as language.

It's only natural to leave the physical behind a while and only natural to return. We live in this physical world as dolphins live in the sea. They cannot live wholly in the medium of their movement, either. They have to rise and treasure up what sustains them in breath-sized amounts from a brighter, infinitely high-ceilinged otherworld. There they touch light raw, but only for an instant. They bear that snatch of the other world down into the resisting water, and it sustains them. Most of us are like that when it comes to the holiest place within ourselves. It is impossible to dwell *only* there, but impossible, too, not to return there. Only saints and mystics go there to stay, and it shows in their tendency to abandon their families (like the Buddha) or never start one at all (like Jesus).

The rest of us leap up and come back down. Dolphins are mammals like us and can't stay submerged their whole lives. Their need to ascend, if only periodically and briefly, is one with their need to breathe. They evolved from land back into water. Their physiology refuses to forget the bright and airy world of their origin. As for people like us, our own origin is in a world above our own, though embodiment keeps us down here. We surface every so often, and we call that meditation, or prayer, or *kirtan*, or reading, or a visit to the temple, or even just a conversation with kindred dolphin-souls breaking through the waves to take in a breath alongside us.

Sometimes a pod of dolphins makes a gray-blue tumult, their rapid repeated arcs approaching a state that, equal parts splashdown and takeoff, cancels out into almost-flight. That is why the faithful like to congregate. Almost-flight is what happens when Brahmins or monks chant verses together, or when musicians play devotional music together, or when you leave your shoes at the temple's bottom step—one pair lost among hundreds, instantly anonymous, everyone raptured aloft together. . . . In time, the Kabir *bhajan* ends, or the paragraph finishes, or you come back down the temple steps to look for your wandering or maybe stolen Nikes. That is the dolphin swimming underwater again. That is you returning to the world where you actually live, and groan over trig, and get told to put away the cereal box, and run out of breath before you run out of run. But you have grabbed a little sustenance for the time between ascents. You have that bit of the bright beyond to last you. On the inside, and maybe on the outside, too, you are smiling the natural smile of the dolphin.

The First Surgery

THIS FIRST SURGERY PUT the first artificial tube inside your body. It was 3.5 millimeters thick and made out of Gore-Tex. It ran from one of the branches of your aorta down to your right pulmonary artery. Non-oxygenated blood poured through it, following a simple high-to-low pressure gradient. (The aortic blood is under higher pressure because it has to go so much farther, all the way out to your fingertips.) Once the blood got into the pulmonary artery, your lungs received it and oxygenated it. If you think about it in terms of trucks and pomegranates: this is a shortcut from the highway to the orchards.

That shortcut wasn't a permanent fix—everybody needs a main road from the heart to the lungs. But it would do for the time being. (Remember which side he sewed to the shunt: right, not left. This little detail is going to matter later, in a big way.)

The procedure is called a "Modified Blalock-Taussig Shunt," but the full name ought to include the name "Thomas" in it. That was the last name of a black man, Vivian Thomas, who perfected the procedure on dogs and even retooled the hemostats for use on babies. Thomas had never studied past high school, but as early as his twenties, he was rerouting canine vascular anatomy. His hands did everything but the first operation on a human being—during which he coached Dr. Blalock while perched on a stool, his face just behind and above the surgeon's shoulder, like a counseling angel. When the time came to give the shunt procedure a name, the white male surgeon's name came first, and the white female cardiologist's name came second. Vivian Thomas did his work in the racist America of the 1930s and 1940s, so his name was left off. The hospital had him on the payroll as a janitor.

This first surgery is also the first time your life is outsourced to a machine.

Ventilators are commonplace. A glorified bellows pushes the lungs full of air, then lets it out. Everyone who gets a major surgery gets a breathing tube down the throat.

The bypass machine is different, and it does exactly what it sounds like it would do: it cuts your chest out of the circulatory loop. Your heart doesn't pump blood, and your lungs don't oxygenate it. The machine draws blood from your body through one fat tube, oxygenates it, and sends it back through another. The bypass machine, roughly the size of four stainless-steel kitchen sinks, gets wheeled into place and parked. A perfusionist stays beside it the whole time.

The surgeon tried to do your shunt procedure without using it. Going on bypass is dangerous, even when the patient isn't all of nine days old. Your heart slowed dangerously every time he tried to work on your arteries, so he had to switch over.

One of the first things they did was cool you down, drastically. Cold blood reentered a cold body. Colder temperatures ramp down the body's metabolism, so your body uses less oxygen. We all sense this relationship at some level, which is why one word for *relaxed* is *chill*.

All the processes in your body slow down their rates. Imagine turning off the gas flame under boiling water; the surface goes calm. Controlled hypothermia scaled your body down, in degrees Fahrenheit, from the normal upper 90s all the way to the lower 80s.

> Ohio snow. A mouthful gives your
>   blue-tinged lips their shiver.
> You sink three feet and keep on falling,
>   miles from our calling.
> Bare branches twist away and bleed,
>   your vein tapped, and the sap sweet:
> You winter, with your switched-out pith,
>   by a snowfall-muffled path.
> In cold white light, your surgeon, welding
>   snowflakes, doesn't melt them.
> Your breastbone cracks, an ice floe
>   sailing from his knife's glow.
> I tell myself: This isn't painful.
>   His body is its own snow angel.

Dr. Z

YOUR MOTHER'S RECOVERY after the Caesarian section had not been easy, and for the first few days of your life, she saw you only rarely, pushed to your floor in a wheelchair once or twice a day. After the surgery, you were still in no state to breastfeed, but she came to hold you and give you pumped breastmilk from a plastic bottle with a nipple. One day, after the nurse helped transfer you to her lap, I left for the apartment to wash up, and she was alone in your room.

After she had sung to you and rocked you a little, she turned to find someone sitting in the rocking chair next to her. She had not noticed this man enter the room or sit down. He was rocking thoughtfully, hands clasped in his lap, with the hint of a grandfatherly smile on his lips. The man wasn't wearing a white coat. For a moment, he seemed to be testing out the rocker, and then he started chatting with her about the names of her twins. What did "Shiv" mean? What did "Savya" mean? And how was she feeling?

How wonderful that the hospital sends around volunteers like this, she thought. She hadn't known how much she liked having someone take an interest in you for your own sake. You weren't just a patient; you were also a newborn boy who had received a name you would keep for the rest of your life. It felt good to be reminded of that.

Presently a nurse entered and asked this kindly gentleman a question about prostaglandin dosage. He answered it with an exact number, still rocking. Your mother, astonished, saw, for the first time, the name tag clipped to his breast pocket: Dr. Kenneth Zahka, MD. Pediatric Cardiology.

I first saw Dr. Zahka years before, when he stopped by the Chest Radiology reading room. Our dungeon consisted of about five or six workstations, giant setups of outsize, high-resolution screens that provided the only light. I was a rookie, a first-year resident, dictating into the voice recognition software. I overheard him two stations down, joking with one of my supervising physicians. A couple of young doctors or medical students stood behind him. He needed to see an MRI study on a toddler with coarctation of the aorta.

I remember noticing his voice right away. Deep, but without aggression; deliberate and slow, but intelligent, as though each phrase had been thought out; warm, but with an undercurrent of humor or wit, as though the very next thing might be a joke, but a joke at no one's expense. I paused my dictation to glance over.

I had never seen him before, but even by the ghostly light of the monitors, he looked more than just friendly. He looked *familiar*. Sitting in his office years later, as the parent of his patient, I would wonder if I had experienced *deja vu* in reverse that afternoon—if I had recognized him prospectively as someone who would become important to me later. To force a rational analysis here, I think his face linked up with a face from my past. His nose, mouth, and chin match, uncannily, those of Nick Farr, my best friend from elementary school. And, of course, it's possible I really *had* seen Dr. Zahka before, maybe in the hospital cafeteria.

Whatever the reason, I liked him three years before I met him. I even recall thinking how that man was born to be a pediatrician, how a kid wouldn't feel scared at all to go see someone like that. I thought about his specialty, too: complicated as hell, and the hours were probably terrible. I wouldn't get *any* writing done, I thought, if I'd become a pediatric cardiologist.

And so I returned to my job, which consisted of saying sentences, rapidly and clearly, into a handheld microphone, which heard and transcribed my diagnoses as coldly as I delivered them: right upper lobe pneumonia, left lower lobe mass.

I suppose Dr. Zahka is a good takeoff point to talk about the people around you.

None of this happened in a vacuum for us. Your mother and I were never alone—not before, not during, not after. Your mother's younger sister lived with us for weeks before your birth, and the two sisters (themselves more than once confused for twins) went about the business of readying the apartment for you and your brother. She even cooked for us, the complex and the simple and the simple made complex (like the peanut butter and jelly and cinnamon sandwich). Barely two weeks after delivering, your aunt drove in from Indiana for the baby shower, then drove over a second time for the delivery. My memories of bouncing and shushing you or your brother at some crazy hour are always cut short by one of your four omnipresent grandparents appearing magically and telling me to go back to sleep.

But the crowd was bigger than that. Your cardiologist was a Syrian Ortho-dox Christian; your pediatrician, a Jew. Your first cardiothoracic surgeon was the son of Egyptian missionaries, and he was training two fellows, one a Bangla-deshi Sunni, the other an Iranian Shiite. The day shift nurse we grew closest to was a white nurse, a Catholic; she was relieved at night by a young black nurse, who was Baptist. All of them were caring for a Hindu infant of Indian ancestry. A Vietnamese Buddhist friend from med school, whom I hadn't corresponded with in years, emailed me out of the blue that week because he'd randomly seen a poem of mine in a magazine. I spilled to him by email what was going on because he was Peds Onc and knew what it was to see a child suffer. His name was Phoenix, the bird said to rise from its own pyre. All of America found its way to you—which is to say, all the world.

To this day, I have trouble staying cynical, ironic, twenty-first-century-writerly in the face of real life. If I transcribed the sequence of your caregivers into a novel, exactly as they came together, it would read as too programmatic, too message-driven about diversity, too sentimental. The longer I live, the more I see life defying the conventions of literary realism. The believable is what has proven to be, in my experience, untrue to reality.

Consider your hands. Consider the pulse oximeter on your index finger, your fingertip inside it, transilluminated red. Now imagine the light coming from your finger, not the clamp. Imagine your whole body like that, the stranger's blood inside you, glowing. (You have undergone surgeries during which you received so many units of blood that, hematologically, you *were* your donors.) Think about all the other hands that have done anything related to your sur-vival. Whose hands invented, tested, perfected that pulse oximeter? How many hands were involved in the construction of the hospital? How about the ar-chitect's firm that drew up the plans? What about the suppliers and truckers who loaded and drove the raw materials to downtown Cleveland? How many nurses have touched you with their hands? And what about the cardiopulmo-nary bypass machine—its inventor, who lived way back in Stalinist Russia; the perfusionist; the company execs; the perhaps preternaturally dexterous jani-tor sweeping that company's headquarters? What about your surgeon, and the surgeon who trained him? Consider the whole lineage of heart surgeons, going back to Alex Capellen, a Norwegian, back in 1895—what about all *their* hands?

Or your mother's hand, when I first held it? What about the hands that had knit your cap? Or the hands that had pushed your bassinet from the OR back into your room? Or fitted the wheels onto the cart, back in the factory? Or, way back before history, invented the wheel?

Connect the dots out far enough, and maybe *everybody* would be included. Hands glowing red, arms, bodies glowing red. Consider how these far-flung secretly-illuminated people might well be "God"—this anonymous, unrecognized, collective, industrious world of hands. One pair of hands spot welding something ten years ago, a different pair taking notes in Human Phys eighteen years ago, a third pair arriving right now to switch out your IV fluids—*these* might well constitute the Mysterious Ways of a working God. God's ways may not be mysterious at all; they may well be human, as the *Bhagavad Gita* says,

> with many an arm and torso, many a mouth and eye.
> I perceive you in every direction, unending in form—
> No endpoint, no midpoint, no source of you can I perceive.
> Lord of the cosmos, your form is the cosmos.

Homecoming

WE HAVE BROUGHT YOU and your brother home to the apartment for the first time. It's much darker here than the ICU; this is the darkest it's been since the womb for you. Just a nightlight in one corner and the digital display of an alarm clock, blinking since a power flicker days before, everyone too busy to reset it.

The apartment is across the street from the hospital and one block away from a dangerous part of town. One of the first recognizably deliberate sounds you and your brother will make will be a mimicry of sirens. They wake you up sometimes, fading out by the same Doppler effect that was used to measure your flow velocities on the echocardiogram. A pale red emergency glow, serried by the closed blinds, pans across the opposite wall. Briefly, it illuminates the two co-sleepers packed into the bedroom.

The loudest sounds in the room right now are you and your brother breathing. It isn't a snore, which scrapes in and slides out—rather a steady, back-and-forth, grunty hum, engine-like. You are twice as loud as your brother. Your parents lie awake, listening to you. It's your first night home. Is it normal to hear this kind of loud breathing from an infant?

Your breathing sound cuts out abruptly. That *can't* be normal. I leap from the bed and bend over your co-sleeper, inspecting you, feeling for breath. You are as serene as death. So I poke you, and you stir. Your lips pulse for a few beats, suckling in a dream.

"Everything okay?" your mother asks me.

"False alarm."

She and I lie in wait side by side for the next wake-up. I find myself smiling at the ceiling. Was there really nothing to worry about? The surgeons have said they will wait for you to gain weight before going in for the final repair—a year, maybe a year and a half. It seems far enough away for me not to think about it tonight. In fact, it is possible, in that bedroom crowded with four whole human beings, to *relax*.

Your breathing changes timbre every so often, but so what? You've got a thin red line down your chest, but so what? It doesn't even hurt you when we pick you up. A sliced breastbone simply doesn't bother kids—it's like nature *made* that bone to be longitudinally divided for easy access.

Is this really all there is to it? After all that nail biting and doomsday echocardiography, all that genetic counseling and abortion-talk?

"I can't believe this is real," I say giddily, propping myself on an elbow.

"I know."

Your mother is trying to sleep. I'm keyed up, exhilarated, like a condemned man just read his reprieve. If only someone had told us! That was the medical advice I would have liked to hear. "Listen up, you two needlessly nervous parents. There will be two weeks of scary-looking machines and IVs and crying, but they'll go by fast and seem pretty hazy even while you're living them. Shiv won't remember a thing, and Dad, someday you'll have to more or less *interview* Mom to figure out what happened. Two weeks, and then you'll be home free—sleep-deprived, and dragging Glad bags full of diapers to the trash chute, like parents of twin infants the world over. So relax!"

We did. And so we began to coast. Those were good months.

A

Miracle of miracles, the King of kings
awakes us with two cymbals, doubling
    nuclei, cochleas, embryos, boys.
They hear their mother humming them to sleep,
two chests of treasure in her castle keep.

B

Miracle and miracle, king and king:
We're ruled by double vision, doubling
    baby Bjorns, co-sleepers, Enfamil, boys.
We do twice the bobbing on half the sleep,
too spent to treasure these strange hours we keep.

Your cheeks got as round as your brother's. We took a picture of you and then your brother being given a bath, and to this day, we can hardly tell apart the smiles. The only difference is that in one picture, your mother keeps the blue washcloth dunked, and in the other, she has raised it to cover the pink weld line down your breastbone. We successfully forgot everything, except your daily half-dose of baby Aspirin.

We could marvel at you and your brother at last, side by side. Identical twins! Rarer than just identical, actually. You and Savya are identical twins, but as we learned after you were born, you are actually part of a special subset called "mirror image" identical twins. Fraternal twinning happens when two sperm enter two eggs—the siblings just happen to be in the same womb at the same time. Identical twins divide one life between them, and each half is a new whole. *Take fullness from fullness, and fullness remains.* If the split happens before nine days (mystical three times mystical three), the twins aren't mirror images. If they split a little later than that mark, the twins are conjoined ("Siamese") twins.

If the twins split in the golden window—later than purely identical twinning, but just before Siamese twinning—the twins invert each other's image. So you have your bald spot on the left side of your head, while Savya has his bald spot on the right. You stayed together until the very last moment.

A

Were you two one self, halved,
Or selfsame, summoned twice?
I love dividing forms.
The merged egg quickens, splits,
Two, four, sixteen, and on
Towards infinity

And past infinity
To the shape it will have.
The nurses set you on
My lap, sliding the two
IV poles past the lit-
Loud monitors, your form

Almost your brother's form,

Only infinitely
Savaged, saved, breastbone split
Like an ice shelf in half.
One love, cloven in two:
You took the suffering on.

Love and mitosis have one thing in common:
They split to redouble, form begetting form.

B

Were you two boys once one
Before you donned these forms,
Or were you always two
Distinct infinities?
Even if you were halved,
What you gained from the split—

As the DNA unspooled
Behind the amnion,
And the two complete halves
Of you took human form—
Was the infinitude
Of being one and two.

You are you, and you, too,
Your souls, synonyms, spelled
Out as *Infinity*
And *One*. Twin hearts—but one,
Not yet in flowing form,
Drained, knifed, sliced in half.

Half infinity is still infinity.

How We Coasted

FEBRUARY, MARCH, APRIL: The good months, mystically as usual, were three in number.

Of course, they weren't all good. That's just how we remember them. The facts contradict the soft-focus and warm lighting. You fought hard against your mother's attempts to feed you, turning away, biting down, breaking the seal of mouth and breast. Your brother, who had been offered the breast since birth, gave her just as much trouble. I was at one remove from those epic struggles on the nursing pillow. I would take one twin out to the main room while she tried with the other. Her mother was with her, fortunately, to attend to that whole mysterious process.

While the attempts seemed frustrating and noisy enough, I'm a guy and didn't understand how traumatic this was for her. Heavily made-up La Leche League matriarchs made it no easier when they stopped by on a house visit. They wore reindeer sweaters and carried large purses and surely had begotten, in their day, spherical male offspring in rude suburban health, since grown into state-champion defensive linesmen (thanks, no doubt, to four straight years at the teat). When they pressed your mother, in their genteel but fanatical way, not to give up, not to give up, never to give up, they only stoked her guilt and shame. The pamphlets they left extolling the virtues of breastmilk made your mother feel she was denying you something you would need to recover and thrive after surgery.

New mothers are prone to depression naturally, even after a totally normal pregnancy. She stayed above that threshold but came close. Throw in sleep deprivation, a thousand (*two* thousand) new things to do, and a body stretched and slit open and sewn back up, and that is one definition of "coasting."

*

As for me, I had to study for a test. Sounds trivial, I know. I would love to tell you how, introduced as I had just been to the Perennial Mysteries of Birth, Fatherhood, and Mortality, a certification of minimum competence from the American Board of Radiology meant nothing to me. Having learned What Really Matters in Life, I regarded my forthcoming oral examination as a trifle.

If only. Your father was not so noble, wise, or philosophical. This exam was Checkpoint Charlie, the rifles and barbed-wire gate leading from the starved, gloomy East Germany of residency to the flush West of a radiology practice. (This is, I realize, a historical reference that you, in the year 2023, are going to have to Google.) Failure, beyond the frank ignominy of it, would have forced a whole *second* year of studying, of digging under the wall with a bent spoon. I knew myself well enough to know I would go at the exam's near-infinite material even harder the second time around. I imagined missing a whole year of watching you boys grow up, reading, and writing.

I wanted to pass that exam worse than I wanted to write. I shut down all my literary activities for five straight months, something I had never done for any test before. Not-writing would be my prison, and in that prison's weight room, I would pump up my radiology skills.

The exam had a whole mythology surrounding it. Radiology residents from around the country drove or flew to Louisville, Kentucky, every year to a specific, slightly musty hotel that had hosted this exam for decades. The Board reserved entire floors. Residents went from room to room on a timer. These rooms were the same rooms where your illustrious, textbook-authoring examiners were staying; you could see their baggage and smell their coffee and smoke-tinged tweed jackets as you sat down at a computer screen. The poker-faced examiner refused all feedback, usually flipping from image to image as you pointed out findings with a regulation coffee stirrer.

Those images were the terrifying unknown. Rumor had it that the images were all arcane. Rumor also had it that the images were all basic. Rumor further had it that the images *looked* basic but were actually arcane to trick you.

The examiner penciled your scores on a pad. A bell sounded. You moved on to the next room, subject to subject.

Sounds benign enough, these many years out. The ABR has since gotten rid of this exam, not least because residents were known to pass out or vomit from the anxiety, sometimes on the examiner's bed. The months before Louisville were a relentless series of review sessions, PowerPoint lectures, self-quizzes, online searches, and stress-induced loose stools. Our superiors, after four years of exploiting our cheap labor, knew the helots were restless and absolved us of afternoon duties for six months straight. One of my fellow residents prescribed himself a beta-blocker and a sleeping pill.

Because memories are not the same as facts, I, like your mother, remember those three months as the months we "coasted." Even that "we" is misleading. By May, it wasn't even true of you.

Baby Boy Blue

YOU HAD PLUMPED UP, cheeks hemispherical and slightly rosy. The clicking car-seat buckle threatened to pinch your thigh fat. You didn't latch onto the breast, but you did latch onto life.

Paradoxically, that worked against you. Your body was growing, and with it, your body's air thirst. Sipping oxygenated blood through a 3.5 millimeter Gore-Tex straw just wouldn't do. Your body wanted mouthfuls, lungfuls of air to bathe its capillary beds. The shortcut couldn't accommodate enough trucks.

Your mother had intended to take you boys to California, where you could see your grandparents and great-grandparents while I, back in Cleveland, would finish studying for my exam. The exam was in early June; I would get one month of total isolation to concentrate. After taking the exam, I would fly west to meet her, and we would visit a half-dozen key nostalgic places in the Bay Area, this time pushing a twin stroller—Carmel, the Botanical Gardens, a specific Thai restaurant in Berkeley. We wanted to visit, as parents, the places where we had fallen in love as teenagers.

A few weeks before the departure, you started changing color.

> Baby boy blue,
> cyanosis oasis blue,
> blue at the lips but flushing pink
> until the pink and blue make
> royal purple, blue blood,
> true blood, blueprint
> of my baby boy
> folding me
> an origami
> blue flower

to stop me singing
the fatherhood blues
for my skyborne
son, my avatar
arriving to dye
our lives
out of the blue
blue,
midnight you, cerulean you
with your Arctic lips
ashiver, breathing and breathing
yet breathlessly blue, you
with your heavenly
changeling's
Krishna hue.

At first, it happened only when you cried, but the tinge around your lips was unmistakable. Cyanosis comes from the Greek word for blue, but the natural pink of your lips made it closer to purple. During these spells, you probably experienced no pain or feelings of suffocation. We studied your lips and hands and feet. These peripheral areas were the first places your body deprived of oxygen. More crucial blood flow, to the brain and heart, bowel and liver, stayed open at their expense. The capital kept itself supplied while the provinces were allowed to starve.

A trip to see Dr. Zahka revealed a blood oxygen saturation lower than it should have been. This first reading was already under 80%. It would have to be watched. If the California trip was in two weeks, could you be seen again in one?

Again the glowing red pulse oximeter clamped your finger, and a reading showed up on the monitor. 76%? Let's try that again, it can't be right.... 74%? Was the machine working correctly?

They fetched a second unit. We made a third visit. Somewhere in there, you had another echocardiogram, sitting curled up in your mother's lap, the clear jelly smearing your chest as it had once smeared your mother's belly. You cried through the rolling and sliding of the probe on your ribcage in spite of *Dora the Explorer* on a side-table television. Even EKG leads terrified you, mere stickers though they were.

Only Dr. Zahka could calm you down. Later, when you were older, he would do it with pictures of his dog on his iPhone, or by turning the bell on his stethoscope. At this stage, before you had language, he did it purely with his voice.

That same voice, gone serious, advised us to cancel everything. Your mother stayed in Cleveland but relocated to my parents' house. More room, more help with food and putting you and your brother to sleep, and most importantly, two physicians in-house, around the clock. Your grandfather rustled up an oxygen tank using his hospital connections, and your grandmother picked up a pulse oximeter. You had a little clinic set up for you in my old bedroom.

Your mother gave me updates every afternoon while pushing you boys around the block. I took the final phone call, I remember, in the Kelvin Smith Library stacks. Fifteen days before Louisville: I had built my textbook barricade deep in the scientific regions of the Dewey Decimal System, safe from the allure of Ariosto and Wolfram von Eschenbach. I put the phone to my ear, and the titles of the dusty books came into sharp and sudden focus. In a strange coincidence, I found myself staring at textbooks from the 1980s and 90s, and they were all about flow, laminar and turbulent. The latest reading, she told me, was 64%. *Fluid mechanics. 532.4: Mass, density, specific gravity of liquids.* 64% didn't just confirm the downward trend, it made "downward trend" an understatement. The echo had confirmed a problem with how the blood was going through the shunt. *532.5: Hydrodynamics. Turbulent flow: Diameter of pipe, velocity, viscosity.*

Dr. Zahka had given us his cell phone number. It was time to call it.

We weren't the only ones with a trip planned that summer. Dr. Hennein had scheduled a trip to Egypt, a charity trip he made every year to operate on underserved children. So just as you approached a critical level of low oxygen saturation, the date was approaching when you wouldn't have access to your surgeon.

Dr. Zahka admitted to us, months later, that he applied "gentle but persistent pressure" to have your surgeon cancel the trip and operate sooner, rather than wait until autumn. In the end, it was the surgeon's decision. He canceled his trip.

I could have felt guilt that my child should draw his wonder-working hands away from the children of strangers, children with identical or even worse problems, who couldn't go down the street to the Cleveland Clinic and get the same surgery. This thought, I assure you, never occurred to me at the time. All I thought was: *Thank God.* And also: *This must be worse than I thought if the surgeon's not going to Egypt.*

The date you ended up going back to surgery was May 20th. You were three days short of five months old. That was the earliest date they could give us; it happened to be my birthday. I agreed to it right away. Magical, religious, and superstitious kinds of thinking surged in me. Nothing bad could happen to you on that day. The surgery would have to go well because it would be too flat-out cosmically strange for a son to code under the scalpel on his dad's birthday. Stories simply didn't play out that way, not in fiction, not in real life. By agreeing to May 20th, I would protect you. I would bind fate's hands.

I remember hanging up the phone after setting the date. I happened to be in the Pediatric Radiology reading room, where my colleagues and I were getting mock exam questions. A case would be brought up on the screen, and one of us would have to describe the findings and propose the diagnosis. I stumbled back in a daze, and the examiner, one of our nicest attending physicians, gave me the next case. I felt lightheaded, as if I had never trained in this field or even attended medical school. I saw, in this ribcage, a creature scuttling and many-legged. What if a centipede had a skeleton? Wouldn't it look like this? The ribs would be legs. Or maybe some hybrid Triassic insect with a rudimentary scorpion-tail—the common ancestor of scorpion and centipede, sacrum and coccyx its curled stinger—

"Hello? Doctor, would you care to take this case?"

I nodded and began to speak. I recalled the template of a Radiology Case Discussion. I simply filled the vacuum with words. The words and sentences did not, when considered rationally, belong in those places. They belonged there only musically. After I had completely botched the case, the examiner revealed, hesitantly, the answer: PA-VSD.

I had, in a sense, failed to diagnose you. There seemed to be a message in this, a reproach. I walked home to you that afternoon with a lightheaded, out-of-body feeling.

The Hands of Hani Hennein

TUESDAY, MAY 20th, 2008. Your second surgery was the last one Dr. Hennein performed on you. Your third surgery—yes, your third; read on—would be done by a different surgeon. We would learn, at that time, how Dr. Hennein was "escorted from the hospital." No one would have any details why. By the time you needed your third surgery, he had started a new job in Wisconsin.

I want to present him as someone superhuman, but Dr. Hennein was only human, like you and me. His first name was Hani.

In 2014, when I was writing about the first surgery he did, I realized we never even sent him a thank you card. I looked him up online. There were plenty of articles about the famous pediatric CT surgeon. Dr. Hennein shot his wife in the face, nonfatally, and himself in the mouth, with a different result. He did this two years, almost to the month, after he operated on you. Google turned up one picture of him, very unlike the professional pictures in a suit or in scrubs.

In the mugshot that is still online, his face is drawn, his gaze pointed a degree down from the lens. Not in shame, more like a man focused on the near ground, trying to make something out as it approaches his feet. The mugshot came from an arrest a few weeks before the gunshots. He had been arrested for domestic assault and battery after striking his teenage daughter "twice on the head, using his hand."

Shortly after the arrest, his wife filed for divorce. The neighbors, tapped for anecdotes, as usual, said they had seen him only once, pacing his garage, talking to himself. He was always elusive like that, even after the surgeries. We saw his nurses and fellows, only rarely the man himself.

He ended his day early, around seven in the morning, in the garage. His two younger children were at home. A Saturday morning, naturally: he had no parents waiting on him.

Those same hands remade the heart that is in your chest. Remade hundreds of hearts, on two continents. He was most famous for his work on hypoplastic hearts, too small and undeveloped to function. Hearts the size of a thumb, or a bullet.

To reach into an infant's chest and correct what nature got wrong, and then to come home to a defiant teenager: Hani would cross a threshold, and his powers would vanish. These few people—his family—knew him, defied him, denied he was any sort of savior.

Or maybe it was the opposite. Maybe Hani spent too many hours working miracle after miracle. Families (like ours) didn't look at him the way they looked at other doctors. All day, he sensed people mapping Fate and Providence and all sorts of cosmic things onto him. Keeping his distance, he mimicked, against his will, the elusiveness of God. He kept mum as much as possible, but it only made him seem more transcendent. Our awe isolated him. He owed everybody else's suffering this show of total control. So he acted sublime all day. Everything un-sublime, everything downright toxic in him, built up in his famous, healing hands. One day, those hands struck someone. They struck someone he loved. And in the end, his hands turned on himself.

Hani had grown up in a family of Egyptian missionaries. That was why he kept going back there to operate. I can see how dexterity and focus and everything else that goes into making good art can coexist with a bad temper and violent hands. Maybe charity, like art, is willing to overlook personal foibles or personal monstrousness. Maybe it's interested only in finding a conduit into the world.

But by thinking of it this way, I attribute the action to the action itself. I take the beauty of that action away from the man who performed it. That isn't fair to Hani.

I do the same for the shooting, the ugly action, when I insist he must have been profoundly ill. His wife, in one of the articles, reported that he had recently stopped taking "a prescription medication." I assumed, immediately, that it was a psych med. That would absolve him of the ugly action, taking the agency away from him and giving it to the illness.

It's still an attempt to reconcile the grandeur and the horror—by taking one or the other away from him in some way. The whole sense of a discrepancy, I guess, comes from the notion of character. A person has a certain character, and this or that action can be "out of character." The notion comes from fiction and movies, where the fake people are even *called* characters, and from religion, where a person is "judged" at the end of his life, as if he were all one thing.

We may yet come to realize that the brain—and all the memories, emotions, contrary motives, desires, resentments, ideals, and fears that constitute it—is as complicated, and as intermittently consistent, as the weather. Mania is an Arctic summer. Depression is a nuclear winter. You don't have a character, you have a climate, and that climate changes.

His first name, in Arabic, meant *happy*.

The last time I saw him, he was in green scrubs, a surgical cap on his head, between surgeries. His visits lasted only a few seconds, and I got up to shake his hand. He must have thought I had a very weak handshake, but I felt his hand was something too precious to grip with force. I treated his hand as I might a hummingbird.

To be honest, I wanted to kiss his hand, and I doubt I was the first parent to want that. The hand was very dry, and nothing set it apart as special.

That was the hand that fixed you in 2008. That was the same hand that would go on to fire the gun in 2010.

Both events are in the past, and I cannot unknow them. The hand I remember has both actions in it. Tigress teeth can rip into prey or pick up her cub by the scruff. There is no contradiction.

There is only the hand that is, and in my imagination, I am holding it. It refuses to alter any fact of itself to honor my notions of consistency and logic. I know what this hand has done. There is no contradiction. My memory of this hand can coexist with the new knowledge. I am lowering my head, Hani Hennein. I am pressing my lips to your hand.

3

REMAKING YOU

The Second Surgery

A

Keep rising, rising higher than the knife
that you are going, going, going under
at half a year old, breastbone sliced through twice.
Keep rising, rising higher than the knife
that's carving Shiva from a block of ice.
Beat hard, and pulse with Himalayan thunder.
Keep rising, rising higher than the knife
that you are flowing, flowing out from under.

B

Keep flowing out from under, through and past.
Become all rivers in full flood, all rain.
Ride home on the shoulders of whitecaps as they crest.
Keep flowing out from under, flowing past
Kailása, that has held and holds you fast,
Shiva your sieve, ravine, your radial vein
that's flowing out from under, through and past
and home to us alone here in the rain.

YOUR HEART WAS MADE ONCE, by week four of your gestation. By
month four of your life, it was remade. Dr. Hennein gave you a "main road" from
your heart to your lungs and blocked off the shortcut he had put in earlier. He
also fixed the hole in the wall of your heart.

First came the induction. That word, when used by an obstetrician, means
medicating an expectant mother so she gives birth. Anesthesiologists use the

word when they medicate patients into a state resembling death. A gas that looks like air, a sedative that looks like water, a paralytic that looks like milk, and . . . oblivion. . . .

Your lungs stopped expanding on their own. A tube stuffed down your throat pushed air in and out for you. (Your cries would come out hoarse for a week afterward.) Dr. Hennein untwisted the metal wires in your breastbone, left there after the last surgery. What had sealed up, he slit again.

Just like last time, your body was cooled down, and you went on bypass. The tubes drained your heart empty. The heart has arteries that supply the muscle it's made of. A potassium solution, injected into those little arteries, fried all your heart's circuitry. The heart muscle stopped contracting. Your heart quivered in its cavity, stunned, unable to pump.

Brain, limbs, lungs, heart: at this point, all your power grids had blinked out. You were still alive, technically, because blood was still flowing inside you—but even the blood flowed only because a machine pushed it through you.

The first task was to tie off your Blalock-Thomas-Taussig shunt at either end and snip it out. Quick work. After that, Dr. Hennein's gloved hand dwarfed the heart it cut into. Fileted open, your heart revealed the hole in its midline wall. A Gore-Tex patch sealed this. Next, he implanted a 16 millimeter tunnel between your heart and your lungs. This conduit is an "aortic homograft," which is a fancy way of saying it comes from the chest of a dead stranger. It is a gift from the dead to help the living live.

Anyway, that was the surgery. Done! All it took was a paragraph.

All it took was eight hours of OR time.

All it took was 111 years of surgical and technological development.

All it took was the whole history of medicine from the ancient Egyptian priests who weighed a heart against a feather, through Galen's imaginative theories of circulation taken as truth for centuries, to the *De Motu Cordis* of William Harvey in 1628, to an operating room in Cleveland, Ohio, in the early twenty-first century.

All that is left is to close you up.

Which they can't do. You come back to the surgical intensive care unit in critical condition, with IV milrinone forcing your heart to beat, and with your chest still open down the middle. Dr. Hennein, trying to shut what he had opened, could not pull the rip's two edges close enough to sew. Any attempts to pull harder made your blood pressure drop dangerously. Your right ventricle has swollen, leaving your heart too big for your chest to contain. In the Operating

Room, after realizing the case couldn't hold the contents, Dr. Hennein laid a slip of sterile Gore-Tex over your heart. He would have to wait for this swelling to go down before closing you up again.

Your mother steps into the room carefully, eager-afraid to see what has become of her six-month-old. Your chest looks like a loaf of split-top bread. The split goes deep, all the way down to your heart, which keeps up a lively twitch at the bottom. A total of fourteen catheters or tubes are going in or out of you. One tube breathes for you and has been taped to your cheek. Another disappears into your penis, a few others into your chest. Thin catheters burrow into your arm veins. She sees you suspended in a cat's cradle between no one's hands. You aren't resting *atop* that crisscross-cradle of string. The strings are running right through you.

Holding you is out of the question. The raw, twitching Gore-Tex graft that covers your raw heart-meat—a few millimeters between this precious organ and the air—makes it seem dangerous even to touch you. She ventures to stroke the exposed skin between the taped IV and the hospital wrist band. You have been remade, but mangled in the remaking, altered utterly. You have come back unexpectedly plump. It's not some optical illusion or wishful vision. Your whole body has fattened the way a sprained ankle fattens. The same swelling that kept your chest from being closed has caused this astonishing inflation of your body. Doctors call it *third spacing*: Your body's 70% water is supposed to stay inside your blood vessels or individual cells, but because of the operation, the fluid has squeezed out into the rest of you. Your flesh itself is waterlogged. Her eyes are fooled, and willingly. Under all these tubes, in spite of this pulsing fissure in your chest, you grant her a glimpse of what you will look like years from now, when you are past this. It will be a few days yet before your chest can be closed, a few days more before you are halfway to semi-conscious. In the meantime, we stare at you. I pace the room. She prays.

Your Open Chest

I WROTE A PAIR OF TWINNED poems at your side, while you lay un-closed. You will see that the poems don't have punctuation marks. That isn't a lack or a defect. I jotted down the phrases, the rhymes, the images, and they felt right at the time, during my study breaks in your hospital room. I haven't gone back and inserted dots and dashes and commas. This is just how these twins came out. Maybe that unfinished aspect matches you as you were then. So I have left these poems as I found them.

A

I see your ribs   your ashen head
the chest tube wound   where you have bled
sacred blood   from your sacred heart
and it's beyond my hybrid art
to reawaken from his rest
the mountaineer snowed under   this
swirl of living funereal ash

O Innocent atop Kailash
a private famine   your samadhi
instill now   in your still-life body
a will transcending mere desire

Come rise & revel in a sphere of fire

B

I see your ribs   your fallen head
the chest tube wound   where you have bled
sacred blood   from your sacred heart
that all their science   all my art
can neither reach   nor resurrect
your scorchmark tongue   your thorax wrecked
ribs of a ghost ship   snapped & lost
planks of a Son   roped in a cross

You bare your heart now   breastbone split
& I bear witness   to the twitch

heart muscle   missile in a silo
Lift off   & thread your solar halo

In the first twinned poem—I'm reading back here, into my own early work—I see Shiva in you. That's why your head is *ashen* in the first line. The word *ash* in English must have called to its Sanskrit off-rhyme, *Kailash*, which shows up some lines later. In the second twinned poem, I see Christ in you. Maybe that's why your head is *fallen* in that poem's first line, the way Jesus's head lolls to the side on the cross. That's also where the "sacred heart" comes from. I remember seeing the same image in the house of an elementary school friend, and, later, swinging from a taxi driver's rearview mirror: Jesus parting his gown and pointing to his chest, where a heart has been painted in bright yellow. Incidentally, the chest tube scar below your twelfth rib marks the very spot where the Roman soldier Longinus, in a medieval fresco by Fra Angelico, prodded Jesus with a spear to see if he was still alive.

The median sternotomy was knocking about in our species' imagination long before cardiothoracic surgeons pulled it off. You find open-heart surgery elsewhere, too, if you look. The Prophet Mohammed's Night Journey to Jerusalem and Paradise starts when the archangel Jibril visits him. The Prophet is asleep. The archangel removes his heart from his chest, "washes" it, and replaces it in the cavity. Going through that purifies him and prepares him for the holy itinerary.

A CT surgeon cuts open a chest and bathes a heart in light. A CT scanner bathes a chest with ionizing radiation and builds a heart out of light. Two means to the same revelation. In your ICU room, I studied CT images of chests and hearts. I denied myself the images of poetry, but they troubled me anyway. Rilke: *The tongue between teeth, the heart between hammers.*

I look back over the book I have written for you, and I see I am writing to you about science one minute, mythology and religion the next; history one minute, personal stories the next. Everything at once. During those scatterbrained hours I spent studying in your ICU room, occasionally jotting down couplets without the time to punctuate them, disciplines interrupted one another. Stress left my thinking disorganized. I could not keep these fields in their separate departments. They linked up like strands of the double helix whose expression we are. This was what I learned at your side: how to experience, in harmonic overlaps and skewed dissonances, a greater beauty than mere internal consistency. Leave consistency to the mathematicians. We are biological integrals. Our elegance is found in our hybridity.

Reawakening

YOUR EYELIDS PART.

Your optic nerves come back to life, but dimly, more a wan glow than a live-wire crackle. You still have a lot of sedatives in you, keeping the neuroelectric voltage low.

All you see is ceiling, standard rectangular panels with one panel throbbingly white, two tube lights behind it. Even if you wanted to look around, you couldn't. Your head is staked in place by the tube in your throat.

Your ears come back on. Testing, testing, one two three. You hear something breathing next to you, a deep breath and a sigh, over and over again, strangely steady and much too loud, like the snore of some sleeping beast. It's a breathing machine: a machine, breathing. You are not alert enough to connect its breath rhythms to your own chest's rise and fall.

Which is just as well. A panic, not to mention the most frantic gag reflex ever, seizes people who grow aware of the breathing tube. It doesn't matter that they aren't drowning, or that the machine is gently and rhythmically mimicking what they would do for themselves, if they could. Ventilator patients require a certain amount of sedation not to "fight the vent," that is, not to gag and wrest back control of their own breathing, even if they aren't strong enough to sustain it.

Knockout drugs in your system keep you from fiddling with your body's controls, from swinging your limbs and pulling these parasitic plastic worms out of your arms. The drug that forced your heart to beat has been stopped, but the rest of your body is on autopilot. A tube drains your pee as soon as you pee it. Your bowels haven't moved in days, partly because there's nothing in you, partly because the bowels get stunned after surgery and can't muster the dozens of little squeezes that push things along. Another tube drains a pink, watery trickle from your chest.

You are surfacing. Blurs organize into faces. You recognize these faces. These are the same people who used to pick you up and kiss you and hold you. Here, so close, is your mother. Those are her lips against your forehead. Why isn't she picking you up? You rediscover your voice. It hurts because the breathing tube lies hard where your voice is, but you have no way to communicate other than to take control of the air pushed into you and force it out. You cry around the tube, and your voice precedes you into the world again, calling the nurse from the nurse's station, and the doctor from a neighboring room.

You have broken the surface. You are back.

Pain

TREATING PAIN IN AN INFANT or very young child is guesswork, in part. Pain gets tricky even with adults, whom we ask to grade pain on a scale of 1 to 10. Does a "7" mean the same thing coming from different people? What if you hear "7" from a protein-shake Cro-Magnon man who faints at a flu shot? From a woman who's undergone four natural childbirths? From a known addict, flagged for narcotics-seeking behavior in the past?

With the extremely young, doctors don't get a number or a description, sometimes not even a location. The most common sign of pain, crying, is also the sign of hunger, the sign of *I want Mommy*, the sign of sleepy, the sign of indigestion, the sign of fever. To complicate matters further, there are drugs that take care of pain, drugs that take care of fever *and* pain, and drugs that simply calm a kid down.

Imagine someone is screaming in pain, and it's your job to make him feel better. The only indication you have of how bad he feels is how hard he's screaming. So your endgame is to get him feeling better, but your end*point* is getting him quiet. You can either dull his pain or dull his *consciousness* of his pain. This is the difference between pain relief and mere sedation.

During your recovery from the second surgery, these two things got confused. You felt thoroughly beat-up and miserable, in a general sense. So you cried. You may have felt pain in some places, though we had no way of knowing where, and you had no way of reporting where. So you cried. You had some mild fevers after the surgery, nothing too concerning, but enough to make you uncomfortable. So you cried. Your sleep was interrupted, and you were hungry. So you cried. There was a mess of reasons why. Your discharge note mentions "some irritability," a phrase which, as any parent of an "irritable" child knows, rather understates it.

You had the tube taken out of your throat the day before I left for Louis-ville to take my big exam. I kissed you for good luck and drove south in our gray Prius; jibbered my way, early the next morning, from case to case, room to room, with a totally blank mind; and drove back late the next afternoon, believing I had failed the whole thing. That was a long drive up I-71.

When I got back to Cleveland, you had just been brought home. The sunlight was weirdly intense, the yellow in it turned up, falling on you and your brother napping on the queen bed, flanked by pillows. You looked identical in that light. I put one finger in your palm and one in your brother's and felt them close. Later that night, I almost killed you.

You had been on a benzodiazepine, Ativan. We had been given a prescription for the same drug in a dose low enough to administer at home, without constant in-hospital supervision. Your mother hadn't had a chance to fill the prescription that morning when she brought you home, so that afternoon, having just driven back, I took the prescription across the street to be filled. Your grandparents offered, saying I should rest, but I wanted to go for a walk and be alone.

I spoke at a window with a pharmacist or pharmacist's assistant, I am still not sure which. She wasn't wearing a white coat and had an air about her that seemed civilian-like, unprofessional, though I didn't think much of it. I sat through a long delay, eavesdropping on two elderly women who sat in the chairs to my right.

"Then as soon as he stopped," one of them kept saying, "that's when it happened, that's when it happened, as soon as he stopped."

Over and over, she said this. It was like she was hugging her knees in a cor-ner of her mind and repeating one fixed obsessive traumatic regret. I convinced myself this was a signal or communication from beyond. These women were messengers who bore a warning. I even had a prickly feeling on the nape of my neck. It was all very surreal. Fortunately, this riff of magical, somewhat paranoid thinking was cut off by the reappearance, in the window, of the pharmacist.

"We had to reformulate this," she said, "so the dosage stapled to the bag is wrong. You should look at what's taped to the bottle."

Or maybe she said: "We had to reformulate this, so the dosage taped to the bottle is wrong. You should use what's stapled to the bag."

I nodded in spite of my feeling this was a setup for disaster. She sensed I hadn't quite registered anything, and she explained it to me again. In retrospect, it seems irregular, or flat out dangerous, that the pharmacist would preserve an erroneous slip of dosing directions, on the bottle *or* stapled to the bag. Why not just tear it off or black it out with a Sharpie? This was, after all, a benzodiazepine prescribed to a four-month-old. The memory of that moment remains dreamlike, as does the Ford Taurus that nearly hit me on my twilit walk back to the apartment. Into the refrigerator went the Ativan, white paper bag and all, in a dream sequence, and the next thing I knew, we were all in bed, and the house was pitch dark, and you had just woken up screaming.

"He's due for his dose," your mother murmured.

I stumbled into the narrow corridor that served as our kitchen and read the tag stapled to the bag by the refrigerator's white light. I stuck the given syringe into the bottle and, squinting at the marks through sleep-stuck eyes, drew back 1.2 milliliters to squirt into your mouth.

To my puzzlement, the whole syringe was full. In fact, I needed more than the whole syringe since it was a single-mL syringe. I tried to draw up more, but the bottle was empty. I took one step toward your bedroom, groggy but perplexed, my mind working very slowly. These were 0.1 milliliter increments on the syringe. Was the dose 0.12 milliliters? Zeroes, ones, and twos got mixed up in my brain. I shook my head of sleep and remembered the warning.

The two wrappers, on close inspection, turned out to be identical—and they both bore the larger dose, 1.2 milliliters. I turned on the kitchen light and stared at the full syringe. You were still waiting, wailing in the next room. The instructions seemed to state I should give you the whole bottle. Had the pharmacist just been too lazy to repackage the drug?

I admit I said some cuss words that I won't set down for you here. Drawing up a sliver of fluid, 0.12 milliliters, I vowed to make some fiery phone calls the next morning. Worst case scenario, I was underdosing you, but better to juggle you overnight than calm you permanently. Because that ten-times-too-high horse dose of Ativan, 1.2 mL briefly loaded in the syringe, could have caused respiratory depression, which could have caused global anoxic brain injury, which could have caused diffuse cerebral swelling and herniation, which could have caused death. We would have thought you were having an excellent night in your swing.

Ativan

THERE WERE NO EXCELLENT nights, or days. You stayed thoroughly alive and thoroughly miserable. We couldn't set you down, but holding you didn't change anything. Meanwhile, you were spiking fevers. Not high ones, and no pus oozed from your chest incision, but such fevers could mean anything. A visit to the surgery clinic, a return home, more misery, another phone call, another visit.

At some point in all this, a letter showed up in the mail cubby downstairs. This letter came from the American Board of Radiology. Simply opening up the letter and finding out I'd passed—it was anticlimactic. I remain ashamed of having worried. Of having given a damn about anything else in the universe while you were still suffering.

Anyway, there's one happy ending for you. Too bad it's the one that doesn't matter.

A few evenings later, still miserable, still intermittently febrile, you had to be re-admitted to the hospital. We cut across from the Emergency Department to Rainbow Babies by going through some basement-level tunnels. Carrying you draped over my arms was quicker than waiting for the hospital transport system (as everywhere, chronically an hour behind). Your mother pushed your brother in a stroller. This basement course had us skirting the Radiology Department, and I heard garrulous laughter as we turned a corner. We stopped and stood facing three of the attending radiologists who had trained me. They were dressed up. I realized my graduation banquet was that evening. Their laughter took a moment to stop, since they had not looked too closely at what seemed like just another patient family—two parents, two kids, two grandparents. Then the three radiologists stopped walking, and their smiles froze and went away. I sensed our family made quite the haggard little tableau in that hallway. Misfortune carries its own embarrassment, like a stink. I played down your present admission. I said it was "just a low-grade fever" and "needed a little watchful waiting," and, with a wink, told them to eat some extra appetizers on my behalf. I wanted to guide them back to the mood we had interrupted so there wouldn't be mute gloom after we had passed them.

In the elevator, your mother and grandparents pushed me to go to the banquet. I would only graduate once, there was nothing to do in the hospital room, they could cover Shivvy, go, go. They didn't realize how estranged I felt from all my colleagues. These supposed friends. How grotesque it would be to shake hands that evening! And to say things were okay and go up on stage to receive a framed piece of paper while familiar strangers applauded.

I slept in your room that night. No one in the world meant anything to me but family, kin, blood.

Your mother didn't isolate herself that way. She had two best friends from California who had both ended up in Cleveland, one doing an Internal Medicine residency, another doing an Internal Medicine-Pediatrics hybrid residency. Pure coincidence, or else divine chess moves to protect you, the King.

Your mother also made a new friend in those weeks. On every one of your stays in the hospital, you had the same nurse, Annie. Annie and Ami were roughly the same age, and they treated one another like sisters. Annie treated you as her own, just as an aunt would have. Every shift, Annie made sure the head nurse assigned her to your room. She arranged for a friend, whom she knew to be a good nurse, to take care of you when she was off duty. You were her favorite. Checking you hourly, day after day, admission after bounce-back admission, meant that she ended up with the clearest sense of your ups and downs. The unit doctors and surgical team members saw you once every morning before rounds. At this single point in time, they asked the same questions. Had you spiked another fever? Were you still inconsolable? They had no sense of your *rhythm*.

Annie, by contrast, because she was a nurse, had to chart, box by box, your vital signs, every hour, in pen. She didn't just see your peak temperature but every fluctuation. She also knew a great deal about your medications because she was the one administering them.

So it ended up being Annie who integrated everything. She showed your mother a chart she had drawn, relating your low-grade fevers, your periods of inconsolability, and your Ativan dosage. This dosing could be higher in the hospital, under supervision, but there were limits on how much a parent could give a baby at home. Annie went back into your records and investigated how much

Ativan you had been getting and for how long. During that long unit stay after the surgery, from late May into June, you had stayed on a very high dosage. Her conclusion: You were going through drug withdrawal.

The next morning, during rounds, she presented her idea to the team of residents. And so a very simple solution took care of the problem. A tapering regimen of Ativan, very high to low to nothing, got you back home and helped you recover by July.

We all agreed that Annie would make an excellent doctor. Shortly afterward, as it turns out, she moved up to the next closest position, joining an Ear, Nose, and Throat doctor's practice as a nurse practitioner. I passed her once in the hospital stairwell, and she wore a long white coat, stethoscope around her neck, poised and hurrying to her next consult.

An Omen

Astronauts nine months weightless
    have to be cradled through the shuttle door.
A body is just a spacesuit
    the soul wears into emptiness.

We swaddle our two returned space travelers
    tight in cotton cocoons.
The pressure keeps the starstuff they are
    from streaking home.

AFTER YOUR SECOND SURGERY and its aftermath, you got positively chubby. Seeing you transform like that, we got the feeling, the deceptive feeling, that we were in control of events again.

Domestic coziness was under constant threat with us. That may be why we valued it so much. We certainly seem to have taken plenty of pictures and clips.

Can you tell yourselves apart? You've got a lot more hair than your brother, a mop on top and nothing at the temples. We used to soap it into a mohawk. We took the customary picture of each of you in the plastic tub, getting a bath, just so we could embarrass you during the slideshows at your weddings decades hence.

Here you guys are again, climbing Mount Laundry. We'd dump it out for you fresh and warm from the dryer. Those were the days, shlepping downstairs to the second floor with giant hampers full of onesies. What little mountaineers you were! Socks on your heads like berets. We dug our arms into the dryer, and the drab burp cloths held a heat that felt alive.

Here's us at Wade Oval. This picture right here is a classic, both twins on the grass. You are playing with your shadows, twins playing with twins.

Gong and mallet twins, no sounding this shimmer, these
songs of green silk I slip in my wallet. Why settle

for half as limitless? Double the love, double the life. Two
cherrybombs flashbang on my easeful bookshelves: Twins

worth twice their weight in overnights. Twins
on the furniture, each the other's stunt double; twins

on the driveway, each one calling out his brother's
double dribble. Twins both in the same bunk

by daybreak, head to foot, as they were on ultrasound.
One twin, solo? The left glove left in a lost and found.

Twins conjoined at the funny bone. Twins alone
of all things living never born alone, stereoscopic suns

giving the sky its first glimpse of depth perception.
Baby boy blue: blue baby boy. Twins each with two moles

stamped at the factory to help tell them apart.
Twin towers, rising out of the blue, into the blue.

Twins powering through blue veins to my heart, half
infinity still infinite, empowering my art.

 Listen: Times were good. Your mother bade a relieved farewell to the whole fraught breastfeeding thing. We would bundle you boys into the Prius and head to the bookstore or the farmer's market in Westlake. In July, a few days after you got home, I found out Northwestern wanted to publish my first book. That fall, I also started a Nuclear Medicine fellowship, in the same hospital, right across the street. It was a good gig: I'd write bits of my mythic epic during the slow mornings, go for a swim or workout over the noon hour, then pound through PET-CT's all afternoon—and be home with you guys every day by five p.m., no call, no weekends. We finally flew out to visit your mother's old haunts in California, hitting every site save for Davis and Carmel. When we got back, we settled happily into our precious routine. Gerber-spooning, spit-up-wiping normalcy made that era golden. Too bad it lasted (that pesky triplicity again) all of three months.

There was one minor incident before your three-month reprieve expired. I call it minor, but I wouldn't tell you about it if it hadn't caused me, at the time, a sense of foreboding. It made that false sense of control vanish.

I set you down on the changing table by the window at your grandparents' house. The blinds, spontaneously, detached off the rod. Neither you nor I had so much as brushed them. I was fiddling with your diaper when, purely by instinct, up shot my arm. I absorbed this absurdly loud clatter between my elbow and the side of my head. You saw it all because you were on your back. My eyes never left your face, and I saw you flinch. A moment later, your expression changed to terror. The stack of blinds had come monstrously alive, shuffling and sliding actively over my body to get at you. I jerked my shoulder and batted the stack away, onto the carpet.

You were crying by now. I picked you up and bobbed you and tried to figure out what had just happened. It had been a haunted-house kind of moment, and I swore in disbelief at the splayed mess of blades. I got the sense you were being *targeted*, and I kicked the thing on the ground spitefully to make sure it was dead. You had gone quiet, peering down at the beast, safe. For now.

> When I have fears that you may cease to be,
>> Before you've fed your book-starved eyes and ears,
> Before your shelves, stocked full of memory,
>> Hold, like rich granaries, your ripened years;
> When I have wandered, blundered late at night in
>> Semantic clouds of sacred Sanskrit writ
> And think that you may never live to lighten
>> A foggy passage with a flash of wit;
> And when I feel, fair creature of an hour,
>> That you might pass away like Keats, too young,
> A chance arrhythmia, embolic shower,
>> Playground collapse, the bloodclots in the lung—
> Then terror strips the bookshelves in me bare,
> My poetry and scripture so much air.

Kawasaki Syndrome

WHAT HAPPENED NEXT, to bear out that foreboding, happened a few weeks later. It started out as a medical cliché: fever and rash. Parents panic, and pediatricians roll their eyes.

Parents that we were, we panicked. Your mother raised your shirt and saw patches of red everywhere. The spots were not painful. Briefly, they would go white when pressed, then redden again. The rash wasn't rough to the touch or oozy, no blisters, no pearly-white raised nubs.

We studied your back by the light of the living room window. Your skin shocked our hands with fever heat, and you seemed unusually unhappy. Your distress reminded us of those bad weeks after the surgery. Was this just how you behaved when your temperature crept over 101 degrees? Your brother, when he got a fever, tended to get quiet, slow to move; you got loud and thrashy.

Medically, I had every reason to believe this was a viral fever and rash, that classic cause of unnecessary trips to the Emergency Department. I consulted with your grandparents and aunt, my three always-on-call physicians. The proper treatment was fluids, fever reducers, and time.

Moments after coming to this informed consensus, your mother and I freaked out anyway and drove you to the Emergency Department.

The physician who saw us there was the same physician who had handled your anesthesia just a few months earlier during the second surgery. Apparently, he moonlighted in the Peds ED. He and I recognized each other immediately, but after one glance, he avoided eye contact. To this day, I can remember his face only in three-quarters profile. I kept wanting to share a doctor-to-doctor look of understanding, a mutual, isn't-this-weird moment about the uncanny coincidence of this second encounter. I realize now that we may have made him uncomfortable: unlike all his other patients, we knew he was only moonlighting here, that he wasn't a "real" ER doc. Or he may have felt nervous treating the son of a fellow physician in the same hospital. I myself get uneasy reading the scans of co-workers and acquaintances. Added to the professional apprehension about making a mistake is a second, entirely social apprehension.

This latter possibility, though—fear of missing something—didn't seem to apply here. My not-quite-friend seemed totally unimpressed by your full-body blotchy red misery. Nonchalant, in fact.

This must be an everyday sight for a pediatrician, I thought. Hadn't I talked down panicky parents myself during training? When was the last time I had truly assessed a pediatric patient in a professional capacity? Medical school, third year. The ED doctor gave an unperturbed once-over of your chest and back. Docs like him saw this every day. It was frightening only to us because you were ours.

And so you were diagnosed with a viral rash. The proper treatment? Fluids, fever reducers, and time. . . .

Eleven hours later.

You are crying and have been crying in your mother's lap on the couch, in the crook of my elbow on the upstairs bed, in the swing with music on, around the bottle as you had so recently done around the breathing tube.

You pause only to lick your sore lips, which have reddened and split with fissures. Are they getting worse on their own, or because you've been worrying them with your tongue? No food except for a forced trickle of milk that, refrigerator-cold, seems to scald your mouth. No sleep, except for an hour or so of exhausted semi-consciousness before dawn.

Come morning, your lips are cherry-popsicle red.

We juggle and pass you around during the day, but by the afternoon, the prior day's reassurances wear off. Our perspective on the ER doctor changes. He didn't have the unflappability of greater experience; he had the dismissiveness of *too much* experience. Or maybe he was an anesthesiologist who really shouldn't have been staffing an emergency department in the first place.

Phone calls. We don't think to call Dr. Zahka, who is your cardiologist. (By the next morning, though, he will be involved.) Your usual pediatrician, the one who has been seeing you since birth, is out of town. Her office tells us we can come in to see her partner at the end of the regular day's schedule if we wish. We know he will be another stranger, seeing you for the first time, but he's better than nothing.

Fortunately, this doctor ends up making the call. It is Day Five at this point. The key to the diagnosis is your mouth, redder and angrier-looking than the previous day. He sends us right back downtown to the Emergency Department, but he writes down what he suspects on a prescription pad to make sure the doctors there will think of it: *Kawasaki Syndrome.*

The Odds

IT WASN'T.

It couldn't *possibly* be.

I knew this disease from my medical school days—it was a favorite on multiple-choice tests—and my memory scrounged for every detail that might make this *not* Kawasaki Syndrome. You did fit some of the criteria—but didn't the *tongue*, not the mouth, get red in Kawasaki patients? Strawberry *tongue* was what textbooks loved to show pictures of: a little kid with a black bar over his eyes, tongue stuck out for the camera, raw unnatural glisteny pink with a white speck where the flash was reflected.

I reached for every possible explanation that could exempt you. I was in denial for hours.

Of all the rare diseases to get, how could you possibly, in a universe with any respect for probabilities, get one that targets the *heart*? That telltale "strawberry tongue" was only one of two infamous details about Kawasaki Disease. The other? Coronary artery aneurysms.

What that mouthful means is this. The heart pumps blood to the lungs and body, but it also pumps blood to itself, through three coronary arteries. In Kawasaki Syndrome, a segment of coronary artery can balloon out so it looks like the bulge in a parasite-infested tree trunk. The blood flow reaches that ballooned part and swirls there, where it can form a clot. That bit of clot then washes downstream, blocks a thin branch artery, and gives a toddler the kind of heart attack that's usually seen in old men. Or, still worse, the balloon can pop. A popped artery spills blood everywhere. A popped artery is very bad news.

It wasn't Kawasaki Syndrome, I thought, it couldn't *possibly* be. Even the doctors weren't sure. The diagnosis didn't land on your chart until later that night, perhaps after Dr. Zahka was contacted. My reaction, for some hours, was less skepticism than flat-out denial. You must not have Kawasaki Syndrome "because" your heart could not possibly take a second hit. Too much random catastrophe was packing into too small a chest. How dare lightning strike the same boy twice?

Kawasaki Syndrome is the number-one cause of acquired heart disease in kids. That's right: you already had *congenital* heart disease, and now, by some crazy turn of events, you had gotten the exact pediatric syndrome that causes *acquired* heart disease.

Had anyone heard of the two diagnoses traveling together? Was there a mechanism, an explanation, a relationship?

Your doctors asked one another; asked Google Scholar, PubMed, and Up-ToDate; plugged terms in their search fields, hoping some recombination might call up a case report of something similar happening to someone, somewhere, ever. Dr. Zahka presented your case at the powwow held by all the hospital's cardiologists to discuss strange cases. No one had any insight. According to the medical literature, there was no causation, no correlation.

Which meant that luck, bad luck, was the only reason, if *reason* were really a word that could be used here. Bad luck meant you had suffered two independent chance events, and the incidences would have to be multiplied.

I have done the math, and it turns out you are not one in a million. You are 1 in 6.3 x 10^9.

No one really knows what causes Kawasaki Syndrome or how it does what it does. I found an article that suggests a relationship with humidifier use. You had slept beside one back during the California trip, but it's a little farfetched to pick that out as a cause. Some researchers have found a relationship to tropospheric winds blowing east from Central Asia, and sure enough, there's a higher incidence in Hawaii and California.

The mechanism of the syndrome remains enigmatic. It may be an infection, or it may be an immune reaction. Who gets it and who doesn't is, or seems, capricious—unlike the common cold, which is known to be a virus that passes person to person by sneeze-mist and germy doorknobs. Kawasaki strikes as a bolt from the blue—although that idiomatic expression, I might note, originated with the very deliberate lightning of Zeus.

Doctors know why a kid gets a cold, but they can't really cure it. With Kawasaki, they don't know why a kid gets it, but they do know how to cure it. The treatment involved hooking your IV up to a bag of immunoglobulin, which consists of little immune particles filtered and pooled from the blood of over one thousand blood donors. So even in this case, you had a sizeable crowd contributing to your recovery.

The fact that IVIG worked so well points to the likeliest explanation for Kawasaki Syndrome, which is that it's an autoimmune disease. Your immune system picks out some part of your own body—in this case, your blood vessels—as "foreign," as the "enemy," and attacks it. Your own blood vessels as your worst enemy: there's a certain logic to that.

You began recovering within a day. The stuff flowed into you and worked like magic. Early treatment kept the likelihood of coronary artery problems low. We were sitting in your hospital room, feeling good about how things were going (that is, jinxing things), when the Infectious Disease fellow showed up in the doorway.

She didn't think you had meningitis, but she couldn't be sure you didn't unless and until she did a spinal tap.

"But he's getting better!"

"We know, but we have to rule out meningitis."

I was facing a robotic insistence, as though I had encountered an AI algorithm that didn't care what it would feel like for you, at last feeling a little better, to get another procedure done. I protested, I called your aunt to get another Infectious Disease doctor's opinion, I bit my fingernails . . . and at last, reluctant to inflict something more on you but fearful of leaving the question open, I gave my permission. And so, only a few hours fever-free, you curled on your side in the fetal position.

Flit needle sipping
neurological nectar:
hummingbird, flower

Your mother held your wrists and whispered to you. I held your knees and ankles. The position accentuated the knobs and divots of your vertebrae. A long, hollow needle slid into the base of your spine, and clear fluid filled the hub of the needle, connected to a length of tubing. The clear spinal fluid dripped into a clear vial.

The clear vial fills
its smiling meniscus
teardrop by teardrop

How Could All This Fit in a Single Year?

TIME IS STRETCHY, like a birthday balloon. It can fit in your pocket when there's no breath in it. Or it can swell, rounding its volume until there's half a book's worth of stuff inside it. How did all those breaths fit in a shriveled sliver of red rubber?

> The spot is tender to the touch no longer.
> Old pain won't reproduce.
> Its empire just evaporates, unmapping
> Asias blue with bruise.
> Mercy ensures the nerves remember nothing.
> They always draw a [   ]
> when faced with what they felt. Look up before
> you say your word of thanks—
> you'll see the missing rhyme, the breve that braved
> what never was a rest,
> the lacuna that cradled a cri de coeur
> as vast as the heart in your chest.

You had two echocardiograms in rapid succession: one during your hospital stay, another two weeks later. Dr. Zahka was making sure your coronary arteries hadn't ballooned. You didn't like getting the study, and getting them often didn't make you any happier to get them. But they didn't hurt, and (because they didn't use radiation) they were harmless. Besides, you got to watch *Clifford the Dog* DVDs in your mother's lap, so they weren't all that bad.

Each one of those echoes, by the way, cost over a thousand bucks. I've never calculated the grand total of all your medical expenses, but it was probably a cool quarter-million by age five. Of course, we didn't have to pay these bills.

The insurance company did. Before you feel bad for the insurance company people, consider that they probably turned a profit of $479 gajillion that year, and periodically tried to weasel out of paying things, and had to be browbeaten over the telephone by your daddy copping his Doctor Voice.

Seeing the statements, though, taught me a great deal about costs—things you never learn as a doctor, only as a patient. The IVIG to treat the Kawasaki, for example, looked like water, but each IV bag was worth its weight in gold, literally.

Medicine turned out, to my surprise, to be full of casual or minor things that would bankrupt anybody without health insurance. The price for anything was usually about twenty times higher than my highest guess of what such a service should reasonably cost. So the ultrasound machine, used to scan your heart, paid for itself after ten scans, less than a week's roster of patients. Of course, the person scanning you needed a salary, and the electricity and air conditioning in the room had bills that went with them, and the hospital administrators and security guards and schedulers and maintenance guys all had to be paid. . . . There's something obscene about thinking of a hospital as a business, managing revenue and outlay. Still, the hospital charging these massive sums turned a profit, and the insurance company that paid them turned an even bigger profit. Illness and suffering generates wealth for everyone involved, except the ill and suffering. We call it the "health care industry," and that industry is powered by disease. No industry in Cleveland thrived half as well. Disease was, and remains, Northeast Ohio's most valuable natural resource.

But I do want to point something out to you. Consider who was *really* paying for your health care. The insurance company collected its money from tens of thousands of healthy people, who paid insurance premiums even though they were fine. They were like the blood donors who contributed to your IVIG, or the construction workers and truckers and electricians who built the hospital: Yet another far-flung crowd of anonymous helpers, secretly aglow.

I am telling you about these echocardiograms for a different reason, though. Your coronary arteries never ballooned the way everyone feared. But each echo covered the whole territory: your heart, your aorta, and the conduit, implanted just a few months before. Dr. Zahka checked everything that could go wrong, just in case.

You can probably guess where this is going.

*

Imagine squeezing a toothpaste bottle. If the cap is off and the tube is new, you don't have to squeeze hard. If there's crusty old toothpaste blocking the hole, you have to squeeze a lot harder.

Your heart was squeezing blood through the conduit, but the blood wasn't flowing freely. So your heart had to squeeze harder and harder. The echo measured the pressure inside your heart and found it unexpectedly high.

The heart, remember, is all muscle, and like any muscle, it can get tired from squeezing that hard, over and over again. Even if your pulse stays steady at seventy beats per minute, that's still 100,800 beats per day. A tired heart gets bigger and bigger, weaker and weaker. The higher pressures meant the conduit, or the branches connected to it, had to be obstructed somewhere. The body forms scar tissue naturally, tough and hard—like the scar ridge down your breastbone, only on the inside, around the conduit. That scarring was causing an obstruction, and that obstruction would have to be relieved.

You wouldn't have to be cracked open, Dr. Zahka assured us. At least not yet. A catheter could pierce a vein in the crease where your thigh meets your hip. Once the catheter crossed the narrowing, a deflated finger-sized balloon could slide along it. Inflate the balloon, and it would open the narrowing. A tunnel of metal mesh—a stent—could prop it open.

After you got home from the Kawasaki Syndrome, the cardiac catheterization suite was where you went next. Not right away. You got to come back home for, you guessed it, three months.

In all this medical talk, I'm afraid I've forgotten to mention something that happened two weeks before your cath date: You turned one.

Happy birthday, son.

How soon after being born you touched the limit of the bearable: prematurely, I would say, but when, really, is the right time? Little shocks and little fears, summed across a childhood or even a lifetime, never accustom the mind to the limit. They can't, because the limit is neither an emotion nor a thought. It is the precipice with nothingness beyond and below it. Grown men, athletes, sprinters after glory—their legs forget how to stand there. Sadhus and gurus go down on all fours, their self-transfiguration regressed to a mewling animal. I suspect everyone crawls. The mammal that basked in sunshine for a Darwinian minute drops forward and shuffles back to the sea. So there is no such thing as too young. We are all rookies at facing mortality. But still: you were too young.

Birth held you over the limit, dipped you in it the way Thetis dipped Achilles in the river.

But at your limit, and only at your limit, can you see what is beyond your limit. That is the source of the terror. In love with its own movements, dancing vainly in the mirror that is the closest thing it has to a soul, the mind misinterprets the limitless as oblivion. Really the limitless is what some call *eternity* and others call *love*, but those words, just like *God*, don't suggest enough terror. Just because the mind misinterprets the limitless doesn't mean its instinctive fear is wrong. Arjuna was full of awe at first, when Krishna showed him his Universal Form. But that awe quickly morphed into terror. He ended up begging Krishna to fold everything back into his familiar, human form. We look away from the limitless to this cluttered world of shapes with edges, of walls and roofs to hide the night sky that just keeps going, of linoleum tiles mosaicked across the abyss, of the solid tabletop that diligently holds your hot cocoa until you are ready to sip it again. The baby bawls until swaddled tight. The pressure on all sides calms him. He can sleep.

> It's only at your limit that you get
> To meet the limitless. You have to break
> Somewhere to let
> The cosmos in. A wish, an ache—
> They're not enough. You need
> A gash. The gash must not just bleed
>
> But gush. You need to empty out
> The way bypass machines reroute
> Heartsblood from the heart.
> Your limit is the sole place where an art
> That solaces another's soul can find
> Its first, defining lines.
>
> Didn't Krishna pick a battleground
> To sing in sight of the soon to be slain,
> The only chaffinch loud before the rain?
> There, at his limit, Arjuna heard the sound
> Of ten thousand breastbones, split with swords,
> Sealed again with a salve of words;

And there, on slaughter's eve,
He saw the limitless, and could not grieve:
Infinite of arm,
Infinite of eye,
Creation one enkrishned I—
A peacock fanned at a factory farm

Above the chickens tumbled on the belt
Witnessing beauty witnessing their death.
The suffering has to plunge in past the hilt.
Only a hollow threaded with a breath
Can host the limitless
In all its symmetries.

You started somewhere others never reach.
The scalpel made its breach
When your umbilical crust had just chipped off,
Purplish-black, glassy-rough,
An alien seashell picked up off the beach.
Newborn was old enough

For the limitless to swirl in,
To bear down on a baby's chest, a whirlwind
Drilling for the heart of you.
That knowledge is a part of you,
But I'm supposed to be your father now,
Limited though I am, and tell you how

It's only at your limit that you see
A shattered conch shell spill the sea,
Infinite weeping,
Infinitely deepening
The sacrifice that burns to offer more
Because it learns to suffer more.

4

COMPLICATIONS

Going Under

ON THE NIGHT BEFORE your first cardiac catheterization, we feast you like farmers fattening a calf. We want to get calories in you. You will eat no breakfast or lunch the next day, and possibly no dinner, either, so on the cath's eve, nothing is denied you. *Nil per os*, "nothing by mouth," starts after midnight.

On this night, before your first cath, your mother and grandmother wake you up at 11:50 p.m. to get milk in you. The official guidelines stated you could drink clear liquids, like apple juice, before 6 a.m.; so that's what you are drinking at 5:56 a.m., groggy, eyes still shut, me propping your back while your mother (periodically glancing at the nightstand clock) angles the bottle for you. It's like fueling a car. Ninety extra calories—water and simple sugar—will hardly power you through the next thirty-six hours. The doctor in me knows that, but you have always had a magical ability to make my book learning vanish.

I can only remember your more recent caths. In my memory, you are always older than you were that first time. So right now, I am picturing you at four or five years old. You get a swig of something in the holding bay, something to slow you and weaken your resistance—the soul's requisite sip of Lethe before it may cross the river. You have a fairy-tale instinct not to taste the potion offered you. So you don't take the little Dixie cup from the doctor's hand. You look up at his face, then to the nurse, then to me, then to your mother, who is holding you. All of us adults are waiting for you to take it, and although our faces are not impatient, you can sense that none of us will give up. This is the thing that has to happen for the day to move on. Finally, your father takes it from the stranger and holds it out to you. You take it and look down into the cup. It has the look and consistency of milk. You don't want to drink. We stroke your head, coaxing you.

"Go on, son. We'll get you water right after. Go on."

You swallow the whole bitter cupful, and we grownups relax and con-gratulate you, *great job, great job*—as if giving in were something brave. A second cup of water takes away the taste. Nothing happens right away, but it is in you, and the knowledge of something *coming* is almost scarier, which is why you bury your face in your mother's familiar smell. You push an offered video game to your brother. Let him play. Do you want us to read you a book, Shivvy? You shake your head. You don't even want the Lightning McQueen, which you park on the hospital linen, stare at a while, and stare past.

Your hearing sinks deeper into your ears. You stop holding up your head. You wait. Voices come through a tunnel with daylight at the far end and twilight where you are. You are not "getting sleepy." Sleepiness has something pleasant about it that makes you want it. Right now, the part of you that would get sleepy feels no wish to wake or sleep, do or not do. No draw in either direction.

Your position—one arm and one leg hanging over the side of the cart, flipflop dangling from your toes, head on your mother's lap—is neither comfy nor uncomfy. It's just how your body happened to drape on the objects around it. Your gown doesn't feel so airy anymore. There is movement to either side of you, but you don't turn your head to follow. Your brother's face flashes across your vision, and when it is gone, you notice his lips had touched your cheek. My arms, sliding under the mountain range of you and lifting, break through and stir you up. You adjust your weight on me in the familiar ways, then give up because your arms and legs are too heavy, and I drop a little to adjust my body under the landslide of you. Your mother arranges your arm over my shoulder. She walks close behind, making eye contact with you when, every so many years, your eyes blink.

When you are set down, the table is flat and hard, and strangers weave about, occasionally looking down. Their voices sound like they are smiling, but you can't see their mouths for the blue masks. The only faces left uncovered are your mother and father's, and they, too, dive and rise, kissing your forehead, your cheeks, rubbing your hair; and then you don't see them, or look for them, as a puffy plastic triangle descends on your nose and mouth. You breathe something new, faint, chemical-smelling. *What's going on?* You realize there is a grown-up's hand, a stranger's hand pressing this thing down on you. And maybe your sens-es sharpen in that last moment of the anesthesia induction, and your panic sees with sudden clarity the hairy male forearm, the veiny tendinous under-wrist, the fat glove, the plastic induction mask leeched onto your face, the ice-white tube lights, hands pulling at your underwear. The iodine is cool and wet in the crease of your groin. You do not feel the bee sting of the needle entering, nor the catheter water-snaking up the waterways of you. The lights cease to exist, and so do the room and the strangers in it. So, in a sense, do you.

Epic Hero

IT'S ONLY BY UNDERGOING that we can go under and get at the knowledge beneath the surface shimmer, the flash and spangle of things. One brave
boy in antiquity, Nachiketas, went down to Yama, the God of Death, and Yama
taught him the wisdom of the *Katha Upanishad*, there, in the darkness.

> The sun does not shine there, nor the moon and stars.
> Lightning does not shine there, let alone fire.

More than one epic hero takes a trip down to the underworld. Odysseus,
Aeneas, Dante: going under, to the place of darkness, brings understanding,
transformation, wisdom.

After the cath was done, a nurse practitioner handed us a glossy printout,
black and white. The catheter had injected dye into the conduit serving as your
pulmonary artery. The dye showed up black in the pictures. I knew what I was
looking at: the tree trunk, the split point, the delicate splaywork out to the periphery. The pulmonary artery has the shape of a forked tree, and like a real tree,
it breathes. Shot full of black like this, it was a leafless tree, silhouetted against
an overcast sky.

> Aorta, artery, artery, arteriole,
> arteriole, capillary,
> capillary,
> air:

> Your body is a fractal.
> It branches finely, but its finest branches fracture.
> Find the part of you that's antigravity.

The heart of you is antifragile.

Everything looked fine to me, maybe because I desperately wanted everything to look fine.

"The conduit has a bulge to it," she said, "as you can see. That's because it's pinched tight, right here. . . ."

I nodded. I sensed something apologetic in her voice, but at the same time, a hesitation to spell things out, as if I knew what she was going to say next. She was giving me too much credit. I was not processing this image as a radiologist.

"The surgeon took a look at the images while Shiv was still on the table."

I stared at the dye-filled artery, your little bonsai tree of life. The catheter that shot this dye must be a thread, I was thinking. These surgeons must use tweezers to operate on toddler hearts, like watchmakers.

"What did the surgeon say?" I asked. "What's the next step?"

"They need to go back in."

The epic heroes only go under once. Nachiketas visits the darkness, learns his Upanishadic wisdom directly from Death, and that is that. *Like an embryo, borne safely by a pregnant woman, / Agni hides in the kindling.* Odysseus went under and met the ghost of Achilles, who said he would rather be a slave in the sunlight than king of all the dead. Aeneas went under and saw his dead father. They underwent the journey they had to undergo, and they did it in order to grow, and grow wise. But they never went back.

You were not so lucky. Shortly after the cath, you had to go back under. It wasn't just a brutal first year of life, then ease and recovery and flourishing. A third open-heart surgery, and you weren't even two years old yet. There was no letting up.

This conduit had aged far faster than expected, its "main road" gone ragged with potholes. We had been told it would last you almost a decade. There is a working theory on why it failed so soon. Kawasaki Syndrome does what it does by inflaming blood vessels. Inflammation has the word *flame* in it. White blood cells—think microscopic balloons, jiggly with napalm—roll into artery walls. (Artery walls, by the way, have three layers: there's that number again.) The same process that attacked your arteries probably attacked the implanted conduit. After inflammation "burns" something in the body, the "charring" shows up as crusty calcium and tightening bands of scar tissue. That is why the conduit looked the way it did.

The new surgeon, Dr. Ungerleider, was a tall and wispy-haired old white man with a calm voice. Like Dr. Hennein, he had an air of unflappability, perhaps a prerequisite in that field. He reminded me of the kindly schoolteachers of my Midwestern childhood, and I trusted him immediately. After he opened you up, his gloved hand brought a strong yellow lamp to bear. Scar tissue had glued everything to everything else. The conduit itself looked beat up. Its far end had thickened to a stiff ring, and the length of it had a hard, gritty feel from the calcium encrusting its walls.

Dr. Ungerleider ripped out that conduit entirely. In its place, he sewed an entirely new tube into your chest. While he was working, though, he noticed that the artery to your right lung had gotten very narrow, too. So he fixed the road on that side. He broadened it and made sure your blood would enjoy a broad, even path to the right lung. The surgery took him several hours. When he came out to talk to us after the surgery, he told us the new conduit was made from the jugular vein of a cow. Your mother and I both had the same magical thought. The cow is sacred in Hinduism; the cow is the Mother. This one, we thought superstitiously, would hold up for sure. We could avoid another surgery until years from now when you'd be a hale teenager.

Recovery. This time around, we made it a point not to get frazzled. Your mother knew exactly what to expect: the wires, the machines, the days of unconsciousness. A rolling suitcase, packed in advance, carried a change of clothes, toiletries, a good-luck Ganesha, picture books for your brother, an iPod and its dock, a pocket Bhagavad-Gita, and granola bars. She made a conscious decision to acknowledge her own thirst and fix herself, from the patient refrigerator, cranberry juice and Sprite on crushed ice. Our network of relatives and friends got updates in a steady voice. She was a self-possessed cardiac-ICU mom. You didn't come upstairs with your heart under Gore-Tex this time, so things were already looking up.

On my own overnight stays in your room, I brought my laptop. I had decided I would work on my retelling of an epic poem, the *Ramayana*. There, too, an epic hero gets mortally wounded with an arrow, goes unconscious, and needs a magical herb called the Sanjeevani to be restored to life. Hanuman leaps all the way from Lanka to the Himalayas to fetch it, but he can't be sure which leaf is the life leaf—so he picks up the whole mountain and flies it home. With you unconscious and the CICU dark well past midnight, in the grim green glow of the monitors, I tapped out meters while your ECG zagged in its own rhythm. I worked on my epic poem religiously—but I had no sense, yet, how my real epic hero lay fallen to my left. I had no idea how, years later, I would become your first biographer, the poet of your epic.

Your Blue Horse

DISCHARGE DAY. I CARRY YOU out of the hospital in the early spring weather. You are still in a hospital gown. It is still a little chilly, so your mother lays a jacket over you. At one point, she asks if I want to hand you off. I shake my head. You are more or less weightless.

In the apartment again, we sink with you to the floor, parents and grand-parents all together. I set you on the carpet. No noise from you, no crying. You catch sight of your blue plastic rocking horse, still where your brother left it, next to the television. We watch in awe as you crawl for it on your own. We had thought you too frail to move like that, but here you are, sawed open three times, pumped full of drugs and blood, starved for days at a time, punctured in your groin arteries and every vein that dared show on the surface of you, su-tured and cauterized, mauled and overhauled—but here you are, back on your blue plastic rocking horse. The heart-lead adhesive-gook still sticks to your bare skin, visible where the gown has slipped aside off the knob of your shoulder. Little Steri-Strip Xs plaster your breastbone.

Toddlers may seem weak and vulnerable, but they're the strongest speci-mens out there. They can endure a depth of damage that would break a grown man for the rest of his life, leave him dragging himself across the floor to the toilet, forever pondering his bad luck and his mortality. But a fourteen-month-old? A fourteen-month-old seals up and soldiers on and doesn't mope. Look at you—not half an hour out of the hospital, and you get back on the horse, literally. Little kids have *fight* in them. Little kids are natural-born superheroes. You ride with a totally serious look on your face, as if you've built up a deficit of rocking-horse time and need to meet a requirement. "Giddyup, Shivvy!" we laugh, clapping our hands. "Giddyup!"

I remember that I was reading, or re-reading, the *Iliad* at the time. I re-member this distinctly because a passage made me stand up from the couch.

Hector is fighting Ajax, who hits him right on the breastbone with a giant boulder. Hector lies flat on his back, knocked unconscious, and the other warriors have to fight around his body to keep his enemies from carrying him off.

Apollo, the sun God who is also the God of poetry, comes down to revive Hector. The chest wound is touched, shocked by the God's hand. Hector sits up from his Ativan-induced coma, blinking perplexed in the estranged sunlight. With two fingers, he tests his tender breastbone, cracked down the middle. His stunned myocardium recaptures its rhythm and beats.

The epithet that Homer liked to use for Hector: *tamer of horses.*

Picture the good prince on the plains outside his father's city, years before the war came to Troy. He is a boy talking to a white horse, struggling to get him to trot in a circle, curbing, coaxing, cooing until, with the sun setting behind them, the fear leaves the horse's eyes, and the boy, spry, almost weightless, skips a few paces and swings himself aloft with princely assurance. Do you see them, the boy and the horse he has tamed? At this distance, in the twilight, that white horse looks blue. That boy is not Hector. Tamer of blue horses, that boy is you.

You and your brother were on your feet by then. Parallel play, in which toddlers focus on their toys with their backs to one another, had ended. Twin A discovered Twin B, and Twin B discovered Twin A. You two interacted before that, of course, but when one of you grabbed a toy and the other gave chase in a slow-mo crawl around the apartment, each twin's focus was always on the cellphone or board book. Now Twin A and Twin B recognized each other as infinite sources of play. You were the toy your brother wanted, only you were funner than any toy, more noisy, more unpredictable, always moving. At this point, you had syllables for a few things. Words would wait a few months. Milestones like rolling over and walking—and, years later, losing teeth—would always come earlier to your brother. The lag period matched the sum total of days you had lain unconscious, your body stunned and unable to grow during that time, like grass waiting out a flash frost.

Happy endings, or happy-ending-like transitions, came quickly that spring and summer. College, medical school, internship, residency, fellowship: I was done with twelve straight years of breaking rocks with my skull and could now move up to breaking rocks with a golden pickaxe. My job wanted me worse than I wanted it. At the interview, the president of a major radiology group offered me a position before the waiter came to take our breakfast order.

The job would move our family two and a half hours south. Columbus gave us access to another well-reputed pediatrics hospital, Nationwide

Children's. Our suburb of choice, Dublin—with its palatial recreation center, its green-painted fire hydrants, its municipally mandated green spaces—had little trouble competing with downtown Cleveland's broken-bottle grin. Your mother, my onetime California girl, quickly fell in love with central Ohio and with the prospect of a proper house. I moved the twin car seats out of the Prius into the new silver Highlander, which was hit shortly thereafter by a tornado of Cheerios.

Before we left Cleveland, we bought two sets of alphabet bookends. We gave both "A" bookends to Annie and both "Z" bookends to Dr. Zahka. Your mother also gave Dr. Zahka a pen inscribed with the sentence: *True wisdom listens to the hearts of children.*

I thought such tokens and trinkets trivial compared to what these people had done for you. Your mother told me we weren't exchanging something, we were expressing something. She was right. How can we make the overused words "Thank you" carry intensity? Spoken gratitude has something easeful and anticlimactic about it. Buying an overly expensive gift shifts the focus onto the giver. Paradoxically, a token, ideally a card with your handwriting on it, is the most appropriate thing. What I am writing for you is also a Thank You note to them.

Dr. Zahka was starting a new practice that fall, moving "just down the street" to the Cleveland Clinic Foundation. How could any halfway functional hospital administration let go of a doctor like him? From the perspective of accountants and businesspeople, off somewhere in a corporate office, he was probably just a name and a title—this pediatric cardiologist or that one.

They aren't all created equal. Dr. Zahka asked around and found us the name of a good Columbus cardiologist to take over your care. It never occurred to us or to him that you should keep being seen in Cleveland. If an emergency came up, you would be admitted locally, and it would be crucial to have a cardiologist in Columbus who knew your complicated history well enough to manage you. So it seemed like the obvious thing to do, part of the transition to a new life.

Before we left town, you had one last echocardiogram. We were told the Peds Cardiology fellow would be in to scan you. The door opened, and to our astonishment, our across-the-hall neighbor entered the room. He was an extremely quiet South Indian who had not exchanged a word with us in two years. I knew his face very well because we always seemed to be opening our doors at the same time, either to leave for work or take out the trash. We would give each other nods but never actually converse. The walls were thin in that building, and I suspect he overheard the more operatic 2 a.m. wakeups in our apartment.

Awkwardly now, days before we left for good, your mother and I shook hands with him and introduced ourselves and our twin boys. You studied his face with what seemed like recognition, and you kept still for him.

The report for this last echo makes a rote comment or two about its blind spots. This is standard procedure; I have done it myself as a radiologist. "Left Pulmonary Artery: Not Seen," says the boilerplate form. "Right Pulmonary Artery: Not Seen."

Your new cardiologist, whom we'll call Dr. K, had a good reputation. We took this for a good sign. At least in intelligence, we figured, this new doctor would be a Columbus-area Dr. Zahka, even if we would never *like* anybody quite as much. Your new cardiologist's reputation was so good that he was booked several months in advance, and we had to see his partner for your first visit.

This other doctor, who saw you on your first visit in Columbus, was an elderly Pakistani who took a brief look at your chart, a briefer look at you, and told us to come back in six months. Your mother didn't care for his offhand air. We were used to Dr. Zahka's careful, point-by-point, end-of-appointment summaries. He would write his ideas down with a ballpoint pen as he loud-thought them, and he would give us the paper before we left, maintaining this tradition even in the era of electronic medical records. This new doctor, by contrast, clearly had somewhere else to get to. Did I resent him? Not at all. He had given us six more months to coast! An unproblematic checkup was a gift.

And so we found ourselves back home in our pretty suburb. Grow, little boys, grow. You and your brother paced out the new house in diapers. Autumn. You picked up a russet leaf and, holding it daintily by the stem, you bobbled about the driveway in toddler-sneakers with little red lights in the soles. Winter seemed to start later every year. Halloween night was cold and rainy, but the very next week we had a sunny spell. Colder, colder. Green plaid zipper jacket, rainbow-striped hat with earflaps, and a Velcro chinstrap that never stuck for long.... Three months of sacred normalcy, then three months more, and at last it was time for the follow-up appointment, to meet the fabled Dr. K.

Dr. K

ONE MORNING, DR. K FOUND a new patient scheduled in his 11 a.m. slot. CHD, family just moved down from Cleveland, where they were being followed at Rainbow Babies. Dad was a radiologist? Caution, doctor-parent! On the one hand, he could count on baseline comprehension when he said things, but on the other hand, he'd be under the constant scrutiny of someone who had half-knowledge about his field.

Around 10:55 a.m. or so, thinking maybe of lunch, or the oil change he had to get on his car, he approached the room where you waited in a gown. He took out your chart and perused it before entering the room.

Maybe he thought: wow, all these congenital issues and, *simultaneously*, Kawasaki? This kid is two months of a Pediatric Cardiology fellowship in one neat package. Or maybe he thought: How did I get stuck with this mess? Or: Poor kid, poor no-luck kid. This one is complicated, *and* the dad's a doc. I hope I don't screw this up. Or maybe he thought all of these things. It's almost certain he was relieved to get the history from an educated couple. He could trust the answers he got.

"Have you noticed any changes recently?"

The parents weren't alarmed, so he wasn't alarmed. "Some shortness of breath if he's very active," your mother said, "but he's always gotten short of breath quicker than his brother."

"Is it getting worse?"

"Maybe a little. Nothing drastic. You can see for yourself. . . ."

And he did. Dr. K went through all the appropriate gestures, listening to your lungs, listening to your heart (whose wind-tunnel murmur can be heard without a stethoscope), and asking a few more questions. He knew, deep down, that this was the modern era, and his recommendations would depend on what the echocardiogram showed.

The echocardiogram showed a *little* ballooning of the shunt, a *tiny bit* of leakiness to the valve. No reason to call in the cavalry or the catheters. Not yet. Why put a little kid through anesthesia and a whole procedure when he was obviously doing fine? Weight was a bit low, but his regular pediatrician could worry about that. What was a good time span before the next visit? How about six months? Okay, six months. We'll do another echo then. If it shows a little *more* ballooning of the shunt, a tiny bit *more* leakiness to the valve, we'll send him on to another cardiac cath. For now, though, six months and another echo. We'll see what we can see.

The dream job was staying dreamy, so we decided to settle in Dublin and buy a house. In its study, where I am writing this right now, I made time to write a novel about the Partition of India. Two of the main characters were twin boys, one of whom was born with congenital heart disease. In the novel, the twins were aged seven or so, though my own Twin A and Twin B were still in diapers when I wrote it. It was the first time I tried to write from life.

I had been wondering about your condition's history. What would have happened to you if you had been born in a place, or a time, without access to modern surgery and medicine—say, India in the 1940s? What if "nature" had been allowed to take its course?

In one sense, there is no absolute answer to that question. There isn't much data on PA-VSD before the 1970s, when doctors started tracking your particular condition separately from Tetralogy of Fallot, which is similar but not as serious. I've seen a statistic about a "60% chance of dying in the first year of life." Yet people have shown up to a doctor for the first time at age 20 or 30, after living with severe activity limitations their whole lives—no long bike rides, no taking the stairs if the elevator's slow, no basketball after work.

These people survived because the body can improvise haphazard connections between the aorta and pulmonary arteries. These random, emergency vessels are called collateral vessels, and they crawl over the area like wild vines. They can't oxygenate blood all that well, but they can serve to keep a patient alive.

Accidents of time and geography played in your favor. You were born in 2008, not 1908, and in the United States of America, not one of the dozens of countries where your condition would have gone undetected and untreated. Statistically, there's likely a kid born this very year with the same condition you were born with—only in India, not too far from where your grandparents were born. And that child has to bank on a 2-in-5 chance of surviving to his or her first birthday.

I'm not telling you this to wag my finger and say, "Be grateful!" I'm telling you this so you don't focus on the unfairness of how things sorted out—how you had to be Twin A and not Twin B. I just want to show you a different, even larger unfairness to focus on, one that won't fill you with resentment or aimless anger but rather with a sense of possibility. Maybe even a sense of mission, like Dr. Hennein.

Anyway, your six-month reprieve is up. Time to get another echo, son.

Time to see what we can see.

Another echo—routine for you, at this point. A couple of episodes of *Caillou*, and we had the latest set of data points.

Were they concerning? Dr. K drew us a graph. The graph had three points on it, each a touch higher than the other. His x- and y-axes were bumpy and slightly slanted, not the most aesthetically pleasing sight, but he wasn't there for his artistic skills.

"Nothing is changing all that drastically here," he said, "but I think we might as well get a better look. The pressures have inched up over the past year, so there may be a narrowing distally. They can put a stent across it."

That sounded reasonable enough. Best to catch something like that early. If your heart had to beat against a pinched artery for too long, the pressure, and hence the strain, would add up and damage the heart muscle. This kind of thing happened over time, he assured us, so we could relax and take a few trips we had planned over the summer, then get the cath done in the fall.

The Peds cardiologist who did the cath was a different one than Dr. K, who, like Dr. Zahka, saw patients but didn't shoot dye in them. The interventionalist was a German. We met him the morning of the procedure. He had a hyperalert quickness to his speech and movement, the speed of caffeine without the jitter. He was tall and slender, and so were his hands. I imagined such hands must serve him well when steering wire-thin catheters around hairpin arterial curves. Flitting into the room to introduce himself, he made a good impression on us. I can still remember his face and summer's-end sun rash, though I saw him for less than five minutes.

Our mood stayed good all morning. This was a minor procedure, after all, compared to the chest crackings you had been through. You had little memory of those days. To you, this was just another hospital full of harsh tube lights and strangers in sinister scrubs and OR caps. You knew nothing good could come of this place. You never left your mother's lap, except for a few circuits of the Preop area on my hip.

After a long wait, the nurse anesthetist gave you the Dixie cup full of mellow juice, the first round of sedatives before they took you back to the suite. We stayed with you while the drug took effect. This time, the benzos turned you into Drunk Shivvy. Your mother held you, and I guarded the sides of the cart. Meanwhile, you got loud and remarkably garrulous for someone with a fledgling vocabulary. Drunk Shivvy was a sloppy drunk, limbs spilling here and there with total self-abandon. The first minute of this alarmed us, but a hooded-eyed grin and a string of nonsense syllables set us smiling and then giggling, even as we kept you from lunging overboard. Eventually, you laid back. The unnatural calm overcame you. We must have been more nervous than we knew to seize on this as comic relief.

You faded out in one tube-lit room, and now you wake up in another. From your perspective, the hours between have been cut out, and the only difference is how bad you feel. Still, the feeling is familiar-bad. You feel the same as you felt the last time you woke up in a gown with the white bandage wrapping your arm and the plastic thingy sticking out, wires stuck to your chest, and a Band-Aid crossing the crease of your leg. You feel it every time you bend your leg; everyone freaks out when you bend your leg, pushing down on your knee. Don't they know it's impossible to keep a leg straight forever? Every few minutes, you forget you're not supposed to move it.

These faces around you are familiar, too—but the looks are strange this time. Your mother and grandmother stare at your face as if they can see a terrible wound there. It's like that time you tumbled off the porch steps, and everyone clustered around you. The fear in our looks triggered the tears, not pain or shock. The same thing happens now. You are, like any child your age, porous to moods even when you don't understand the words being said by grown-ups. *Right PA occlusion—trans-atrial puncture—systemic collaterals.* Your father and grandfather stand at a painfully bright window.

The apprehension in the room soaks into you. The panic rises in you and emerges as crying. Either you have done something, or something has been done to you.

What happened?

"There is Nothing There"

YOUR MOTHER AND I had gone home to wait during the procedure. We planned to await the post-procedure phone call and drive back before you came out of the anesthesia.

Your grandparents had come down from Cleveland to help take care of your brother during these days, and your grandmother had kept lunch waiting for us. A physician herself, she always consulted her lunar calendar before we scheduled your procedures. The date had to be auspicious according to the stars. That astrological outlook may strike you as silly, but it is older than most living religions (ancient Vedic priests, like Babylonian and Mayan priests, were also astrologers) and a trippy doctrine if you think about it: This idea that multiple futures exist simultaneously. The zodiac turns slowly around the present. Moving forward under the sign of this or that star, you are stepping down a specific passage to a specific future.

Tuesdays were supposed to be auspicious, and she had chosen this day for you, but she was still full of foreboding. "I just want him to come through okay," she murmured a few times, half to herself.

"It's not some big procedure," her son insisted—the confident radiologist, who had squirted dye into a few arteries himself way back when. "If they find a stenosis, they'll 'plasty it and pop in a stent, and that's that. They do it all the time. He'll be home by tomorrow, Mom. Relax."

Oddly, her son's phone rang within a few minutes of that conversation. He took the call cheerily enough. She watched him from the table.

"Yes, this is Shiv's dad. How'd it go?"

Her son turned and swept into his study, asking a question she didn't quite catch—and the speed of his movement and the way his head lowered told her that something was wrong. She rose from the table with a glance at your grandfather. Together they drifted toward the half-closed study door, through which they glimpsed their son kneeling on the ground before the black recliner, holding his forehead, saying, "So there's nothing there? So there's nothing there?" as he stared into velvet the color of outer space, the color of contrast dye on a fluoroscopy image, the color that is not a color at all but an absence of the light by which colors, arteries, stars are visualized. "And on the right," her son murmured, "there's nothing . . . *there?*"

In this telling, your four grandparents have been intermittent presences, always implicit. Yet they were never one generation removed from your story: They were inside it at two levels, experiencing it as grandparents and as parents. The first focus of their compassion was you, but when they looked up from the hospital bassinet, they saw their own son pale and bearded like never before. After all, their boy had always moved through his life without resistance, according to plan, good grades and a happy romance at nineteen (with a Gujarati girl, no less!) that ended in a Big Indian Wedding, where he and his dad had danced with their ties around their foreheads. Now, for the first time, things were going wrong for their charmed son.

Your mother's parents, too, found their sheltered elder daughter sobbing over the phone every few months. She had lived at home through college, prayed in Sanskrit before every meal, gotten engaged to the first boy she dated, the weather in San Ramon 71 degrees and sunny for the outdoor wedding: now, for the first time, their charmed baby girl had to live the kind of anguish she had figured so exquisitely in her classical Indian dances.

Now your mother joins your grandparents outside the study door, the foreboding contagious. Inside the study, her husband's voice is shaky and strangely loud as he asks, over and over, "So there's nothing there? On the right? Nothing there?" He is kneeling as if to pray, only with his elbow on the recliner seat and his forehead on his hand, and his phone to his ear.

What happened?

> He'll live, they said. Just without two lungs.
> Oh God, she breathed. So young. Too young.

> Breathlessly, I called up heart centers
> In Dallas, Boston, Cleveland, Tucson.

> You're a doc, right? Can you give us details?
> I choked on his history. I was too stunned.

When he had just now learned to walk,
He learned how hard it was to run.

Outside the office, winded maple trees bent forward.
The air conditioning blew cold on my two sons.

My two sons were once one. One twin's been halved.
He'll have this half life, then, two lungs reduced to one.

Think of it as a natural disaster, an earthquake, a rockslide. Rocks and crags have completely blocked off the road to the right orchard. No trucks can get through. These rocks are way too heavy to clear. Still worse, there is no intact road beyond the rockslide. The rockslide has blocked off the entire road, from the right turn at the T, all the way to the orchard. Even worse: It seems this rockslide was even bigger than anyone predicted or imagined. The right orchard is buried under rocks. Nothing can go in, nothing can go out. It takes a long time for the meaning to get through. A rockslide blocks the passage between the ears and the mind.

There is only one artery to one lung now. Your left lung is the only one you have left. You will breathe, from now on, half breaths.

The phone call I took that day around noon came from a nurse in the control room, just outside your angiography suite. An image had been paused on the bank of monitors. Our friend the German, in a blue sterile gown and face mask, studied the same image on a screen inside the room. You lay on the table before him, cruciform, unconscious, eyes taped shut.

The tree of life angiogram from the prior year looked different this time. Back then, the tree trunk split in two and branched out from there. This time, one of those two halves was completely missing. The contrast went from the heart, through the conduit, and curved off to the left. On the right, there was a cutoff, and beyond that, pure white space. Nothing there.

"The procedure is still going on, sir. We're calling to get verbal consent for a trans-atrial puncture to inject the pulmonary veins."

If this sounds like gibberish to you, son, it sounded like that to me, too. "Excuse me?"

"The doctor needs to do a trans-atrial puncture to investigate the pulmonary veins at this point, so we just need your verbal consent to proceed. The arterial injection showed a total right PA occlusion, so he needs to see if there's any venous back-filling."

More gibberish. I focused on the only words I processed, *trans-atrial puncture*, which sounded like they were going to stick a needle through the wall inside your heart (which turned out to be exactly what they did). They knew best; I gave my consent. While I did, some of her other words sank in. Specifically: *occluded*.

I began to realize the dye study had uncovered a huge problem, and the nurse's professional tone was underplaying it. I kept her on the line.

"So, ma'am, about the conduit? They injected that already? And the right side is. . . ."

"There's no flow to the right side."

"It's closed off?"

"Right. It's occluded."

"Totally?"

"That's what it looks like."

"There's nothing there?"

I had rested my forehead on my hand. I raised it now and closed my palm on my sweat. She had answered me, but I had not heard.

"Excuse me, ma'am? There's nothing there?"

She was in a hurry to get off the phone, understandably. I was delaying this last step of the procedure, which was a desperate way of finding out if any part of your right lung was salvageable. If an injection could push contrast back through your lung's veins, back through its capillaries, all the way into an open artery, it would mean there was something left: An open tube that could be hooked up to your heart. This was a long shot, and for all my confusion—if you're confused right now, trust me, so were we—I already knew that right lung was lost for good. It was as though I understood nothing but this one fact.

"The doctor will speak with you once the procedure is over," the nurse said, "which should be in about twenty minutes. He'll be able to explain what happened."

If you had been in the car with us on the drive over, you would have seen your mother keeping her composure and your father bawling. There are places to submit to that kind of jumping-chest cry, and 270 East at 80 miles an hour is not one of them.

"Pull over," your mother said. "I can drive."

I shook my head a bunch of times, both to say no and to shake off the cry. I was okay for a few seconds before my eyes crunched shut on their own again. I swerved and corrected. A few indignant horns sounded behind us.

"Take this exit, or pull over."

"I'm fine."

"You are not safe right now. Your eyes aren't even open. Pull over so we can switch, okay?"

For years, I have marveled at her serenity during that drive—so much so that I brought it up to her before I wrote about this car ride back to the hospital. She shook her head and told me I had never explained to her how final all this was, how you had lost the function of your right lung totally and permanently. The way she experienced that afternoon, the phone call was clearly bad news— it had to be, or I wouldn't be so torn up. The phone call meant you would have to go through some drastic surgery again, but she trusted in your toughness and in the Gods and in modern medicine's risky ingenuities. The possibility of a dead-end diagnosis had not occurred to her, and why would it? Doctors had never yet given us bad news without the promise of a treatment, however scary-sounding. Your mother had hope because hope, until that day, had always been medically justified. What I knew before the angiographer even told me—and what took months for your mother to realize, in part because I didn't have the heart to lay it out coldly—was that this time, the doctors had nothing to offer. They had shaken their heads and pulled all the catheters out.

I didn't end up letting her take the wheel. The last thing the boys need, I told myself, is a fatal car wreck with both parents in the car. This thought alone ended up stiffening my upper lip. I must be careful not to assist bad luck with bad judgment. This steering wheel in my hands was the only thing I still controlled. The rest of the cosmos was property of Chance. Hands at ten and two, I ordered myself. Keep your eyes open, breathe steadily, and drive. No one is protecting you but you right now. Anything can happen.

In the consultation room at Nationwide Children's Hospital, the quick-spoken German angiographer told us what he had found. Your right pulmonary artery had no "other side." Clotted blood packed it solid, from the tree trunk's split out to the farthest, wispiest twigs.

Dead Space

DR. K DID NOT SHOW up that afternoon. I don't know whether he was contacted with the results that day or that evening or what. He knew where to find us, if he had cared to say hi. Around noon the next day, he found his way upstairs to us.

That morning had been quite busy for Dr. K. He studied your medical records more closely than he had ever done before seeing you in his office, something like a student poring over the textbook after he's bombed the exam, knowing in retrospect exactly where he should have focused. He had a powwow with the angiographer, during which, I suspect, they traded litigation anxieties. More than one cardiology colleague was called or curbsided. Best guesses were traded, shoulders were shrugged. Be careful how you play this, his colleagues (probably) counseled him. Get all your ducks in a row. Don't incriminate yourself.

In his preparatory running-about that morning, he encountered—purely by chance—a wheelchair getting pushed down to Radiology for an x-ray. You were in it, sitting in your mother's lap, her hand guiding the IV pole. So the first confrontation happened prematurely, before he had his story together. According to your mother, he barely said anything. No admission of guilt or apology, but not even an expression of surprise or sadness. "If he'd just said it was terrible, if he'd just been like, 'I can't believe this happened,'" she tells me, "it would have gone a long way." But he didn't then, and he didn't later that morning, either.

We had our what-went-wrong meeting in the residents' meeting room. You weren't letting your mother go anywhere, so your grandfather and I met with Dr. K. A couple of scruffy stray residents in scrubs glanced at us and decamped immediately. Maybe they had heard. There was a dry-erase board on one wall, which bore some incompletely wiped-off acid-base calculations. Dr.

K picked up a green marker and drew us the trunk with two branches, the old familiar pulmonary artery, the tree of life that was now half withered.

"So, what we think is, what we're thinking is . . ." he began. Maybe the first person plural referred to how he had consulted with his colleagues before having to face us. Unless "we" was a grammatical mechanism to inflate his authority, in the manner of a bureaucrat or an editor. "This is the side where the shunt was, so this, right here"—he made a dense zigzag over the right branch—"is where he must have scarred down, scarred down and shut off flow there, so it clotted off. . . ."

He was flushed pink and getting pinker. His features distorted under my stare. I saw only his apple cheeks, his bald head with the residual hair in a swath from temple to temple, and this increasingly pink face, as though he were a baby in a white coat. Dr. K kept his eyes off the stares of these two physician relatives. Your father had what must have been a stunned blank expression; your grandfather had an open-mouthed frown that hinted less at skepticism than outright disgust.

"Or the other possibility is," Dr. K went on, "and we went back and looked at all the surgical notes, is, see, this is the side they worked on last time—they said it was narrow, and they put a patch there, which means they widened it. So that's another place it could have pinched off because he scarred down. Right? And there was no way we could see that on echo because it was all the way, all the way out *here*. . . ."

He kept talking, kept reinforcing the zigzag that cut off the right lung from the heart. Your grandfather, the whole family really, wanted this doctor sued and on the street. But I kept thinking: *He must feel like shit right now, trying to explain this in retrospect, how this happened on his watch.* You may notice I haven't named him here, even to you, though I could have. As he spoke, I thought of how he had seen you all of two times in his life, while I, supposedly a doctor, had lived with you every day. I dropped my head and barely heard the futile questions your grandfather started asking. My *watch*, I thought. *This happened on* my *watch.*

> *What Might've Happened* is the book
> whose pages tore us.
> *What Happened* is the book
> spread on the desk before us.

Let the dead read the dead, say the living.

Prospero's books have drowned.
In every book of *oh if only*
God only knows what can't be found.

Breathe, and keep on breathing
in the vise of your ribs, in pain,
after the jab and the dye in the vein
breathe, and keep on breathing

though every breath be halved.
No doctor's plotted graph,
no sprinkle of pixels under glass,
no faith or fate or father have

a say. The past is the only place
there is no choice.
Mine are the memories. Mine the remorse.
Yours is the breath and yours the voice.

I think that the right-sided artery's repair, done the prior year, scarred down and eventually shut off. I think it closed off so slowly you never got short of breath or felt a sharp pain, the way you would have if the artery had closed off suddenly.

Body fluids can change consistency after they sit around. Milk curdles; blood clots. Stillness cues thickening. Fresh clot has a gooey, jelly-like feel. I remember startling at a snot-like streak of it on the back of my glove, my first day training in the angiography suite. Older hematomas harden into blood rocks. Veins clot more often than arteries because the flow in veins is slower, under a lower pressure. Arteries can clot off, too, if they get too narrow, and the flow slows from a whoosh to a trickle. That's what happened to your right pulmonary artery. The blood inside it slowed to a stop and hardened.

Your right lung still inflates and deflates with air, but the air in that lung doesn't oxygenate any blood. The air simply passes in and out. Half of your lifesbreath enters dead space. All of your oxygenation gets done with your left lung, which happens to be the body's naturally smaller lung. This isn't fatal by itself. The twofold symmetry of the body gives the organs and senses a backup. If the left goes out, the right can serve the purpose, and vice versa. You can lose one eye and still see, blow out one eardrum and still hear, donate one kidney and still pee. The doubled lungs work the same way. People do live without a right or a left lung, usually elderly smokers who have had a cancer resected.

The problem with having one functioning lung is this: there's no backup anymore. It doesn't take much to get thrown into respiratory failure. All you have to do is get a pneumonia in the sole functioning lung, or throw a clot north from a leg vein, or take in a mouthful of pool water down the wrong pipe during swimming lessons. . . .

I should have guessed, back then, that you would never get more than three easy months at a time. I never picked up on your three-month rhythm—though now, as I write it, your epic appears to possess a remarkably regular meter. My sense of rhythm failed me, but so did my medical knowledge. What had I been through medical school for, if I couldn't pick up on this slow-motion catastrophe going on inside my own son?

I daydream an alternative way things could have played out. As soon as Dr. K says, *I'll see him back in six months, and we'll see how the echo looks then,* I stand up and shout: "Wait! Something's not right! Let's cath him *right now!*" I make this leap of medical intuition about you. I override Dr. K's passivity and our own wish to spare you another procedure so soon after your third surgery. I make phone calls, I charm schedulers. I lean on the skeptical interventionalist, doctor to doctor, when he claims you can't possibly need an invasive study so soon. I get you cathed and stented the very first week we get to Columbus.

I wish I had saved the day, son. You were elvin-slight but electric, and you used to do a stomp-dance over the new house's carpet, and you belted out a big cry when you got your flu shot that fall. How was I to know, how was I to guess what was happening, when even on half-power you were that explosively alive?

> Memory of pain:
> circadian cicatrice,
> awakening ache

I still saw Dr. K (not on purpose) every few months. He lived in the same neighborhood (we've moved out since), and he went to the same Rec Center to work out. So the only times I encountered him were in the context of physical exercise. Cardio turned that balding head pink and those apple cheeks blood-red. Sweaty but never out of breath, Dr. K liked to ride his bike on the sidewalk alongside his robust children. We would make eye contact and nod. I used to report my sightings of him to your mother, but I stopped after a while. No need to force her back, with a single name, to a place of futility and anguish.

All the errors in judgment, I guess, could be traced back to one big error in judgment, which was letting you out of Dr. Zahka's care. That afternoon, I called the insurance company and demanded to re-establish with him in Cleveland. I was ready to spit fire and phone-thrash some bureaucrats, as I had occasionally had to do amid your early surgeries, when they got squirrely about payment. I kept a book handy to outlast the epic wait-times with which they wore down a caller's patience.

The expected confrontation never happened. Of course we could go up to see him, the lady explained. Zahka, Kenneth MD was an in-network provider and was covered by our policy. "You could have gone to seen him," she said, "from the beginning."

It's pure superstition, of course, this conviction your mother and I have that nothing can go truly wrong if Dr. Zahka is keeping his eye on you. It leads naturally, for me, to the belief nothing *would* have gone wrong if you had kept seeing him. It's hard not to confuse the two. Might he have noticed something? Been more aggressive? Analyzed the arteries better on the echo? Ordered a cath earlier? This has become one more only-if, if-only scenario by which I imagine preventing this, one more pathway to a better alternative destiny.

I guess it depends on the idea of predestination. If it had to happen, it's best it *didn't* happen on Dr. Zahka's watch. This way, he has been preserved for us as your guardian figure. We still have a cardiologist we trust. It's best for him, too: He has been spared the guilt of letting you down.

Hope

WE SENT YOUR DYE STUDY images on a CD up to the Cleveland Clinic, along with your chart. Dr. Zahka showed the images to the interventionalist, a woman who bore the beautiful first name of Lourdes—a place in the foothills of the Pyrenees, famous for miraculous healing. She looked at your images very closely. The Columbus angiographer had only back-injected *one* vein; anatomically, the right lung has more than one. Other veins drained different lobes. The vein that wasn't tested, in fact, drained the right lung's largest lobe. If that lobe were still viable, she suggested, it could be hooked back up to your heart.... The whole pomegranate orchard might not be gone. Almost half of it might still be there for you. Dr. Zahka called us back later that week. After making it clear he wasn't giving us "good news," he explained there might be hope.

If a repeat study showed signs of function in the lower lobe, you would have to be cracked open a fourth time. Your inner plumbing would end up with tubes that connected to tubes. The Cleveland Clinic could handle the cath, but any surgery that took place afterwards would be very, very complicated. I did some research, and so did your grandfather, and so did Dr. Zahka. Two centers in the country seemed equipped to handle an issue this complex: one in Boston, and the other in Texas.

I sent everything—operative notes, discharge summaries, images on CDs—to both places. Texas got back to me first.

To my astonishment, the surgeon himself sent me an email and shortly afterwards called me up on my cellphone. To my further astonishment, he was supremely confident. His down-home twang I had expected from online interviews and videos about him; what I didn't expect was the casually upbeat prognosis he gave me.

"We've done several kids just like him," he began. (I had found zero case reports resembling you.) "We've had promising results. It's a long road, but when they get there—and there are a few surgeries—I've seen kids regain a whole lot of function."

I pressed the phone hard to my ear, shaky all over. My physiology was rejoicing for you, but my brain seemed entirely independent of my pulse. The medical part of me kept nagging at the elated part of me. It was the cold, analytic part of me that spoke. "Even with the artery completely clotted off?" I asked. "What do you do with it? Do you recanalize it?"

"Right, well, we don't do this in an endovascular way. This does involve a sternotomy. We're able to take a better look out to the peripheral branches—"

"So you open him up to 'take a look'?"

"Right, so we take what we find there—and we're not saying this doesn't take more than one surgery. We've been doing some cutting-edge work with exactly this situation."

Cutting-edge—it's supposed to be an attractive, technological word, but it hits different when there's a son and a scalpel involved. I wish I could explain to you exactly what he explained to me that morning, but he stayed vague. I mentioned I was a radiologist and would like to know the anatomical nitty-gritty of what he would actually *do*, but he refused to get specific. I realized, as my pulse calmed and my heart sank, that this renowned international cardiothoracic miracle-worker was trying *to recruit you for a study*. Everything he did would be experimental. From his perspective, your body was a rare find. He could test out, on you, whatever new surgical idea he had come up with. This was how surgeons became world-famous, wasn't it? By taking risks? And wasn't this how life-saving techniques were developed? Someone had to be the first.

I wasn't quite ready to donate your body to science while you were still alive. I challenged him, but not out of aggression. I wanted to hear him reassure me.

"Literally everything I've heard or read," I insisted, "says there's no way to salvage the artery after it's totally clotted off."

"We saw a blush on those images," he insisted. "It's not totally gone."

"Shouldn't we do a cath first, then? To be sure? Before you open him up?"

"Of course, we can do that first. We've got a crack interventional team out here."

Crack: That word! I could not bear that word in this context, when we had just been talking about cracking your chest. I felt increasingly uncertain of myself—and of *him*, in spite of all the media profiles.

The conversation troubled me for days. I told him I would "talk it over" with your mother, but I didn't go into it very deeply with her or with any of the family members who called for updates. I feared sending everyone into a frenzy of hope.

The next week, I had an email exchange and discussion with Boston Children's. The cardiologist there promised me nothing. He recommended that, "just to exhaust all the possibilities," we fly you up to Boston and get one last catheter study, to check every artery and vein of the right lung. Based on the images I had sent him, he was almost certain that the whole right lung was unsalvageable. A cath could confirm that. We should come if we wished to be absolutely sure of the bad news. He could promise that Boston's surgery team would review the cath after it was done.

I talked through both options over the dinner table with your mother.

Texas, the high-risk choice, on the off chance of a reversal. Boston, the low-risk choice, to make sure we were right to give up.

Did we chase the miracle, or seek out a seal on despair? Did we go with Texas or Boston? Oddly, just a month before, on very short notice, your mother's parents moved from California to Texas. This seemed like a clear enough sign. Your mother wanted me to decide. I was the doctor, after all—it should be my decision.

I guess you can spin that as a test: How hard did I *really* believe in signs, in coincidence being secretly meaningful? How hard did I believe in transformative intervention, divine or surgical?

I went with Boston because Boston offered less hope.

One morning, two weeks before our trip to Boston, the operator from Nationwide Children's Hospital told me a doctor wanted to speak to me.

It turned out to be our friend, the German interventionalist.

"There is *no* reason to do another cath," he started, his voice unexpectedly husky, his emotional pedal to the floor. "*No reason at all.*"

"The Cleveland Clinic and Boston both said it's worthwhile injecting the last vein, the vein that drains the lower lobe. Just to check everything."

"They are not going to find anything," he said. "It was completely appropriate, what we did. There is no reason to repeat this."

Doctors in two different cities had reviewed his work and second-guessed him, assuming he was a second-rate nobody in a midsize city who hadn't been thorough—and he was so indignant and so hurt that he was willing to call a parent up and tell him there was no hope, no hope at all.

The angiographer waited for me to respond.

"You did things right," I said. "Boston is just something we need to do before we close the book on this."

"They are not going to find anything," he insisted. "There was nothing there. There was nothing left."

Boston Children's

FAST FORWARD TO A WINTER afternoon in December. We wheeled our bags into a downtown hotel near the hospital campus. The room stayed dark even after we opened the curtains. The sky was pavement-gray, and the pavement was sky-gray. All the buildings around us had been built in the late 70s, when brown brick buildings were designed in the shape of brown bricks. You arrived with a big-immigrant-family entourage: Your mother and father, your brother, and both grandmothers. More loved ones would have come if we had asked.

We turned on every lamp and bulb in the room, desperate to cheer ourselves up with some fake sunshine. You and your brother had already escaped to a bright, cactus-fantastic Radiator Springs. All you boys needed was a bit of floor. You spread out a glossy poster that had a racetrack on it, and you were off to the races. By the time you read this, you will have left the Pixar movie *Cars* behind. In fact, unless you're extraordinarily precocious with words, I'll only give you this book to read when you're getting your own driver's license. Back then, though, your brother always had to be Lightning McQueen, the red racer with a lightning strike on his side, while you were the brown tow truck, Mater—McQueen's buddy, who pulled disabled cars into the garage to get their engines fixed.

You boys kept your cars with you the next morning on the shuttle to the hospital. Patients, or models paid to pose as patients, smiled from advertisements on the sides of buses. Their faces were enormous, each tooth bigger, seen up close, than your whole hand. The hospital lobby had an airport-terminal-like vastness to it, or at least that's how we remember it. Christmas carols were playing ('twas the season), but that only gave the hospital a feel of calculated mirth—like it knew your fears and took this measure to distract you. They were supposed to help people here, but you, with a foreboding of needles, stayed close to your mother.

The cars helped calm you in the hospital lobby, and in the waiting room, and in the room where we waited after leaving the waiting room. "Vroom vroom" was the mantram. Concentration steadied your eyes. It wasn't a distant or dreamy look. It was, rather, a look of intense *presence*. By comparison, we grown-ups looked groggy and bewildered. Your four wheels locked onto the back of a chair or a glossy magazine on a table or the crinkle paper on the examination table, transforming them into pure highway in a pure desert, straight and bright and open, an Arizona of the mind.

You almost certainly won't remember the pediatric cardiologist you saw in Boston. You saw him for one cluster of encounters, immediately before and a few times after this cath. His manner was memorably kind, and I could imagine him being someone else's Dr. Zahka. Pediatrics, I remember thinking, really *does* attract nicer people.

Of course, he was more of a gatekeeper between you and the mysterious experts scheduled to catheterize you, a face for the family to put on the experience—but Dr. Zahka's role, too, came down to this sometimes. After his hands felt for the bottom edge of your liver, pressed the stethoscope to your heart murmur, scrolled through pictures of his dog, gave you the cookies he baked at home, wrote out his summary of the visit—in the end, Dr. Zahka has to hand you over, too. As a clinician, he decides which procedure to do when. Performing it is left to the interventionalist's hands or the surgeon's. So there is always a period when he, too, waits for results, kept outside the sanctum of the fluoroscopy suite, where the high priests enact their mysteries. Your skin is the magical threshold he does not cross. Maybe it's this limit to his power that keeps him human and close in a way no surgeon is—for sometimes he, too, has to wonder What The Doctor Will Say. He becomes, for a while, your third grandfather.

On the day before the procedure, we navigated a maze under Boston Children's Hospital to get the necessary labs and chest x-ray. You are usually a "hard stick." Every surface vein perforated, blew out, or scarred down in the year and a half after your birth—hand veins, elbow-crook veins, even the ones on the backs of your feet. Phlebotomists, like guitarists and poets and tennis players, sort into a natural hierarchy. Skill can take one to the second tier, but only inborn cerebellar elegance gets anywhere above that. Your veins require a Mozart among phlebotomists, and Boston's wasn't even a Salieri. You writhed in your mother's lap, one arm tucked behind her, your kicking legs under my armpit, your tiny wrist manacled between my thumb and forefinger.

Meanwhile the needle stung, withdrew, and stung again. Blood was everywhere—or maybe it wasn't, and only your shrieking makes it seem that way in retrospect. This supposedly routine vial filling was the trauma that would stick in your memory. For at least a year after it, we had to promise you before blood draws that "this one won't be like Boston."

The morning you went under, we deployed, in timed stages, toys, time-wasting apps, and snacks to help your brother pass the time. The hospital lobby, as it turned out, carried an exhibit of original Dr. Seuss paintings. These weren't famous ones from the books we read at home, but colorful, imaginative tableaux and satirical pieces. All the characters bore distinctively Seussian animal faces. Your mother and I stared at these all morning. I tracked down online a list of paintings that were at the exhibit, and neither she nor I can recognize a single one. Distraction must have cordoned off our memories. Our minds were upstairs, with you.

I do remember the winter's first snowfall beyond the busy rotating doors. I walked away from the exhibit to make sure and watched the snow a while. Traffic had built up in the circular drive, and a wheelchair platform lowered from a van, the anthropoid figure in the wheelchair at a forty-five degree slant, expressionless, devoid of muscular tone. Cerebral palsy, I thought. We should be grateful. There are worse fates.

Ring ring: my cellphone was calling us back upstairs.

Too little time had elapsed. All they could have done, the radiologist in me knew, was slide the catheter in and up, squirt, then slide the catheter down and out. No balloon, no stent, no channel burrowed for blood flow to some small patch of still-functioning lung.

No river in the desert, no miracle.

No surprise.

You were still coming out of anesthesia when we got the results formally in a small consultation room. A *This Is Your Body* cartoon poster hung on the wall.

Our gentle, interface doctor was the one who had to do it—the "Boston Dr. Zahka" who didn't really know us but somehow, either through bodhisattva-like universality of compassion or excellent acting, seemed like he cared. This is what they taught in medical school Clinical Skills courses: A Warm Bedside Manner and the Art of Breaking Bad News. Empathy administered by ear to patient and/or parent in fifteen-minute doses. He was good. I was unsure of his first name, but I wanted to hug him. Until he brought up switching out the entire contents of your thorax.

"It's just something you may want to think about," he said. "Heart-lung transplant recipients do remarkably well afterward in the pediatric population. It's a big procedure, but in a case like this, in his case especially, it may be something to consider."

"They do worse, I assume, the later they get it done?"

He shrugged. "It's not a decision that has to be made right away."

Your mother remembers him as "chatting kind of philosophically" about this. I was imagining a stranger's child killed by some thunderclap—and a phone call in the night to Ohio saying they had found a donor—yes or no, yes or no—and then you, on zero notice, after a red-eye flight to Boston, undergoing a cardiopulmonary engine-swap. . . . The solution sounded drastic, the nuclear option. You would have to take drugs that suppressed your immune system so your body would not attack the new organs; Covid was a little under a decade away, unthinkable at the time, but those drugs would have put you at risk. . . . I tried to balance the downside of a single lung—windedness, no athletics— against the risks of switching everything out. The cardiologist explained that windedness was only the way this showed up on the outside. The real danger lay at the heart of you: Your heart was beating against an obstruction through a leaky valve. Every heartbeat, even at rest, took as much work as other hearts did while exercising. Muscles tire. When the heart tires, it starts to fail, ballooning in size and pumping less and less. My mouth went dry as he spoke.

"Just something to keep in mind, that this option is out there," he said casually. Then his serenity stumbled a bit as he spoke and respoke, correcting himself. "They do well. Frequently. They frequently do well." His eye contact broke, and he looked down at his hands, maybe remembering some cases where heart-lung transplants hadn't done well. He added, a little more quietly: "They can do well."

> I thought I'd teach you how the world is changing.
> You handed me a snow globe full of rain.
>
> Water is born with a feel for gravity,
> But falling's the only school for rain.
>
> Thunder away, since you've got the lungs for it,
> But don't expect to overrule the rain.

Who knows if these are bombs or meteors?
Your city bears it like a mule in rain.

We lift, we lilt. Lightning loves a kite.
We tricked the clocks, but we'll never fool the rain.

There's only one way to come through life with honor:
Challenge your fate and fight a duel with rain.

Time

ONCE UPON A TIME, there was a Prince, the Prince of Windsoar, who lived in Windsoar Castle. All he knew of that castle, ever since he could walk, were its stairs. All he knew of play was running up and down those stairs. Naturally, he was out of breath a lot.

On the way up, he looked to his right and saw doors at every floor. But these doors were locked.

"Why can't I explore that way?" he asked his parents, the King and Queen. "I see all these pictures of Windsoar Castle's west wing on our walls, lining the spiral staircase, but I've never gotten to run through the Library of Windchimes, or the Perfume Gallery, or the Hall of Scentiquities, or the Airy Terrace. All those are my birthright, aren't they? And I could use that room to play rather than always playing up and down this staircase."

"They are your birthright, my winded little boy," said the King, "but not everybody gets their birthright just because they're born. The castle's east wing is locked for a certain reason, so just enjoy the rooms you have in this west wing here—your royal bed-chamber and your inexhaustible stairwell."

The Prince played outside sometimes, in a narrow garden. His one ball was always sneaking behind thorns. The other wing of the castle was blocked off by a high wall, and twice, when he tried to climb the wall and peek, his father's half-dozen trained cockatiels descended and pecked at his handholds.

The Prince was getting older, and the bedroom and stairwell and garden felt increasingly cramped. He could not bear knowing there was a whole wing of the castle off-limits to him. How long could they coop him up in this narrow east wing? Even the poorest children in the kingdom had more space to play than a flight of stairs and a garden smaller than a prison yard. The Prince of Windsoar, trapped in his half-castle, thought himself the unluckiest boy in the kingdom. For every other boy had all his birthright, even if it were just a hovel, and every other boy had the run of the fields and the meadows; but the Prince had walls of stately old stones to hem him in.

So one night, at the stroke of midnight, he tiptoed to the top floor's door with a screwdriver. He worked to get the knob off the door, careful not to wake up any stickler cockatiels. Then he fiddled around a little more and got the lock to click aside.

He flung open the door . . . and saw the night sky with all its stars. It was sixty dizzy feet down to a burnt-out set of craters. Moonlight helped him make out the rough foundation outlines of a throne room and a dining hall. To his horror, the crater reflected the moon—it was full of water, and restless crocodiles lurked in it. Here and there, he made out the outlines of poison trees, heavy with dimly glowing blue pears, instant death to eat. Vampire bats burst into the shrieking sky.

"Now you know," said his father's voice behind him, "why the west wing of Windsoar Castle is locked. Years ago, when you were still a baby, a mad King declared war on us, looted our countryside, burned our villages, and bombed this castle from the sky. Only this half of the castle survived, your mother the Queen, and me—and, thanks to you, our Kingdom itself."

"We wanted to rebuild that wing of the castle," his mother the Queen explained, "but how could we do that when our subjects had lost their homes entirely? So we ordered the rebuilding of everything else, and we have made do with half a castle. Soon you will be King, and you can make whatever policies you wish. You can requisition all the stones from all the quarries and make this castle twice or even three times its original size."

The Prince pulled the door closed. "That won't be necessary," he said. "I can live here, and comfortably enough. I never knew how lucky I was. A bomb could have made rubble of this wing, too, the wing where I was sleeping in my cradle—it was a matter of feet and inches. Unless it wasn't luck at all? Maybe God protected me because he had some great dream for our kingdom and for me, and he couldn't bear to see them leveled."

The Prince of Windsoar discovered, overnight, the vastness inside his limitation, the whole extent of his half-castle. He put a fresh coat of paint on the balustrade, and he strung it with lights come Christmastime. He helped his mom replace pictures of the west wing with pictures of the east wing, and they spent an evening making new frames. The Library of Windchimes had been destroyed, but there was nothing stopping him from stocking a new one in his royal bedchamber. For many years afterward, the King and Queen delighted to hear the clear and complex tinkling of his music, and from down the road, judging only by her ears, a traveler from before the war might think the castle stood exactly as it had before.

You may have noticed by now that this telling isn't very good about including dates. I have the dates in front of me, but it feels, paradoxically enough, *inaccurate* to tell you this cardiac catheterization was performed on December 5th, 2011.

You don't remember it in that precise historical way, if you remember it at all. We don't, either. But above all, we didn't experience it that way.

There may have been a moment when we stopped and zoomed out and realized our twins had been in the world for all of fifteen, or eighteen, or twenty-four months. Then as now, the dates provoke a touch of disbelief. I have to count the months on my fingers, like a schoolboy learning subtraction. I don't trust the result I get by mental math.

"They weren't even running around yet," your mother tells me. I've told her about these past few chapters, and she's talking me down from my guilt. "There was no point when we *could* have seen a change. They'd just gotten up on their feet."

I nod, but I'm confused. "I could have sworn he was older."

"How much older?"

"Not a specific age. Just—*older.*"

You're thirteen right now, as I'm revising this passage about timing. I wrote the first version of these paragraphs when you were six. I raise six fingers so I can look directly at how old you were then. I take away three fingers and marvel at the years. Why didn't this whole sequence of events feel more hectic? For any other child that age, I might need a page or so to write a life story, and I'd still be padding. Did you live an epic or a haiku?

Nine straight winters on the march
home to the Battle of Wounded Heart.
This heartbeat, then the next one: He
storms and takes the hills of his ECG,
laughing it off as blood draws speckle
his arms like so much shrapnel.

My child soldier, risen, fallen
under a gunsmoke-haze of pollen,
the order *Suffer* from high command

a paper asphodel crushed in his hand,
epic hero, sole survivor,
enigma I cannot decipher.

No ribbon, no Purple Heart, no star.
Only the Order of the Scar.

No wonder I underestimated how long this telling would get. This was supposed to be a double-spaced letter when I started it (I'm raising some fingers again) seven years ago. Eight pages total, I projected. Type it up, print it out, seal it in an envelope.

Shortly after we returned from Boston, you completed your fourth year of life.

Happy birthday, son.

Where your breastbone has sealed
the scarred skin
glistens

like the fresh-traced weld line
where two sheets
of precious mettle
meet.

All the surgeon did was make a cut.
You're the one
who heals,

you, the miracle-working
metal-worker
in the foundry of your heart.

You lift your welding-helmet on its hinge
as the last sparks, refusing to go out,

converge and settle, slide and pool
in your cupped palms, thick
ahinahina blossom honey

sweet enough to write by,
bright enough to drink.

5

YOUR PEOPLE

Motherhood

I used to calibrate the dome
of her around the edges in our home,
pointing a coffee table out to warn her,
steering her by the elbow past a corner.
Our twin boys sailed in that hot air balloon
of golden skin and would be landing soon.
I felt their heads around week thirty-four.
They nuzzled up into my palm. I swore
I felt the fontanelle, the sentient hole
where memory goes ice-fishing in the skull
for past life images of who they were
before they minnowed the fleshwater lake of her.

THERE IS A WAY we imagine things happening, and a way they really happen. I used to have a superstition—still have, to be honest—that if I imagine an event will happen a certain way, that is the only way I can be certain the event will not turn out. Reality escapes hope the way wet soap slips the squeeze. Not that the event necessarily falls short. Your mother and I each imagined, separately, what love and marriage would be like. I never imagined the nineteen-year-old beauty who strolled with me around Pier 39 in San Francisco. I never imagined the photograph that shows her posing in front of the enormous Christmas tree downtown, squinting into the sunlight, this photograph that's at my elbow in the study where I write this. I never imagined I would send her everything I write, as I write it. Nor did she imagine walking next to me in the mornings, talking through her ideas for her first novel, *The Torchbearers*. We are glad that real life ignored our imaginations. We would not have dreamed big enough.

Naturally, she imagined motherhood, too. One baby to begin with, an idyll that matched the cultural imagery of Yashoda chasing the toddler Krishna. Loud, colicky nights were still theoretical, and diaper changes, in the abstract, are loving and odorless and never require a full bath over the sink. Right away, she got news of two, the blessing doubled, the Gods giving more than she had asked for. That exhilaration was still fresh when she got news of the heart defect, the Gods mixing something unexpected and unfamiliar. Should she worry? She looked to me for signals. Shortly after the diagnosis, I came home from an overnight call shift and told her how I had seen a chest x-ray on a child with Tetralogy of Fallot. At two in the morning, scruffy in scrubs, I had rushed into the emergency department and spoken to that child's mother, sobbing how we had gotten a similar diagnosis, and that stranger consoled me, telling me how her son was doing well and lived an active life. I took this for an excellent omen, and Ami's spirits lifted. Then we talked with Dr. Hennein, and she says I told her, "This is something they repair. You repair it and move on."

So throughout that frenetic first year, no matter what unexpected things happened—even when you split wide open and your heart lay exposed under a Gore-Tex square, and a loop of tape fixed the breathing tube to the cheek she leaned over the bassinet to kiss—she stayed hopeful. She never lost her sense that the Gods were guiding events to a happy, or happy enough, conclusion.

When your right lung closed off, that changed. She had thought you were doing fine. The risky, frightening period was supposed to be over. You seemed in good health before that fateful cath when she learned "there was nothing there," and no one had imagined what it would reveal. Still worse, over the coming weeks, and especially after the Boston visit, she realized this was permanent. Her son had reached, at last, the limits of science and surgery. The loss of the lung broke her sense of cosmic benevolence. Until that event, even the catastrophes and unexpected turns were something to wait out, pray through, give thanks for after she got you back. But now? Our family, it turned out, was not under special protection. Something irreversible had snuck up on you. Anything could happen.

A

Why is this one smaller than the other one?
Because three times before he turned two,
he opened his chest and sent his heart sprinting
to the moon and back. Because God makes

mirror image twins while mere machines make
replicas. Because two apples off the same
apple tree can feel distinct in the palm
yet pack the same sum of sugar. Because
be quiet he can hear you. Because a wrestler's
soul and a dancer's soul weigh just as
nothing. Because we are equally
small from the vantage of the light
that shines on us, and the only eyes
that matter are the eyes of love.

B

Why is this one bigger than the other one?
Because we should all have bigger versions
of ourselves to step in front of us
and make our bullies go pale.
Because two equally sweet oranges off the same
orange tree don't have to be the same size.
Because God was in their details. Because twins
aren't the same people, they're maps
of one another: All they have to do is look
to locate themselves. Because epic
and epigram are both poetry. Because Galileo
proved that two bodies of different weight
fall at the same acceleration
asleep in the same twin
bed. Because mother nature
made sure their mother, in a darkened room
cradling both on the nursing pillow,
could know without looking whose head she kissed
before she set them
in their side-by-side baby bouncers
to float at the same acceleration
up into dreams
identically
infinite.

There's this medieval poem called *Parzival* about the Holy Grail. It's not a cup, as it is in *Indiana Jones and the Last Crusade*, but a stone that provides infinite food and drink. In medieval times, when famine could count the ribs of the dead, superabundance (which we take for granted in contemporary America) was the ultimate blessing. Parzival, questing in the forest, arrives at the castle of the Fisher King, Amfortas. There, at the King's table, Parzival partakes of a feast where the food and drink are infinite. The only off-note is Amfortas himself, who shifts in his seat, malodorous in the agony of a thigh wound. Parzival notices, but no word of curiosity or compassion crosses his lips. The next day, he is sent off into the forest again, to continue questing for the Grail, and it's only later that he learns he had been in the presence of the Grail, he had been destined to find the Grail and heal the Fisher King and gain glory, he had been *so close*—but he hadn't done the one thing he had to do. He had not asked about the wound. If he had said out loud one password of compassion, the Grail would have been his.

Words mean more than we think they do, even token ones. Sometimes, especially, thoughtless words—like the casually curious query, *If you're identical twins, why is he bigger than you?* It evokes a backstory too painful to tell, a query you and your brother play off with a shrug and a smile.

Just as thoughtless words can hurt disproportionately, thoughtful words can, just as disproportionately, help. So your mother knows how much even a brief text checking in can break the loneliness of suffering. A phone call can give the obsessive mind a release valve. The internal monologue, directed outward, lets up for a while. Living through this with you has sensitized her to the suffering of others and given her an understanding of what they need. The people around her know this and come to her. Sometimes while cooking dinner, other times stepping out for a walk with her phone, she listens, she consoles, she gives advice, she brings meals to friends overwhelmed by a hospital vigil, or long recovery, or loss in the family. Part of this, no doubt, is her compassionate nature at work. But no small part is you at work through her. What you have taught her. What you have awakened.

After she published her first novel, she started posting her retellings of mythological stories online, in English and fluent Gujarati. A storytellers' event asked her to share a story "from life," so she combined the stories of two heroes she loved: Hanuman and you. Long ago, she framed and set an image of Hanuman above your crib, the same one that's above your writing desk today. Religious icons encode whole stories in the details. (Radiology studies do the same thing—so a missing blood vessel on the image tells the story of a purple-lipped boy.) Simian Hanuman, Rama's indefatigable fighter, is kneeling. His hands have pulled apart the flesh of his chest. Beside him is a broken string of pearls; inside his chest is the tiny portrait of a man and a woman, both crowned, with their hands raised in blessing: Rama and Sita, incarnations of the God and Goddess, whom he houses in his heart. She took a story from Hanuman's childhood and spliced it with yours. While I can't notate the moving pitch and inflections of her voice, I can place here, as a keepsake, the text of the story she performed.

Leaping for the Sun

By Ami Majmudar

FOUR HANDS, FOUR FEET, two heads . . . all coming in and out of view through the cloudy ultrasound image.

"It looks like they're both boys."

Twin boys? Really?

I look at them on the screen, batting each other through the amniotic membrane. And I imagine my twin sons, playing someday. Running, jumping, flying. And I run, jump, and fly with them. And, as we fly, I tell them a story:

Look at the sun, boys! Doesn't it look like a fruit? It reminds me of a story: once upon a time, there was a mischievous little monkey. He was the son of the wind god. He was climbing a tree when he saw it: the biggest, reddest, juiciest fruit hanging just above the highest branch. He climbed as high as he could and then he leaped: up up up into the sky, which was getting brighter every moment. And when he got closer to the fruit, he opened his mouth wider and wider. He wondered how it would taste: this bright, fiery fruit. When his mouth finally closed around the fruit, the little monkey had time for only two thoughts: 1. Why is this fruit soooooo hot? and 2. Why is it suddenly so dark?

And then something slammed into his jaw and sent him hurtling toward the earth.

It is a thunderbolt, and not just in the story. I am brought back to the ultrasound room with the thunderbolt of a diagnosis: "I'm having trouble seeing Twin A's pulmonary artery," the doctor is saying. "And there's a ventricular septal defect, right there. It looks like Tetralogy of Fallot." Translation . . . there's something wrong with Twin A's heart. Very wrong. He will require surgery. More than one. All open heart.

Instead of planning a nursery theme, we visit the ICU. Instead of taking a pre-baby vacation, we meet the surgeon who will operate on our son's heart. We decide to name Twin B Savya, which means Vishnu, preserver of the universe. For Twin A we choose the name Shiv, the first god, without beginning or end, the first yogi who drank poison to save the world. We question God, the first of many questions: what kind of God messes up a baby's heart? Which God threw the thunderbolt that hit our son? Which God will catch him?

When the little monkey hurtled toward the earth, his father, the God of the wind, caught him. The wind wafted him into a cave, a boulder slamming it shut behind him. The wind went out of the world, and, outside the cave, the little monkey's mother clutched her own chest, trying to draw breath and pray at the same time.

I clutch Shiv, not even four months old, as I walk toward the operating room for the second open heart surgery of his little life. I smell his head, his sweet baby smell pushing the antiseptic hospital smell away. He's content in that moment, his body relaxed in my arms. But when we get to the door of the operating room, the nurses reach out to take him from me. He grabs me tightly with his little fists. It takes everything in me to pry his little fingers open and make him let me go . . . to let him go. This is the one place where I can't go with him. I can't hold him when he will be pierced and lose consciousness, when he will be in a cave, not even drawing breath for himself. The operating room doors close with a click. My son is in open heart surgery.

When your child is in surgery, the nurse calls you every hour. You stare at the phone as each minute passes, willing it to ring.

"He's still in surgery. Everything is going fine."

"He's still in surgery. Everything is going fine."

"He's still in surgery. Everything is going fine."

That last phone call is different though.

"So, he's stable . . . but we haven't been able to close him up. Not yet."

"You can't close him up? What does that mean? Does that even *happen*?"

"Not often, but occasionally we have to do what we call a delayed sternotomy closure."

"But why?"

"His heart swelled up when we operated. It's too big to fit into his chest cavity right now. So we keep him open and sedated until we can close him up again."

I hardly know what to expect when I enter the intensive care unit. My son is, well, he's bigger, pudgy even. His cheeks are fuller; his little fingers are thicker than before. Pink lips are open over the ventilator tube. More tubes stick out of his torso, draining him. And over his chest, which is broader than ever, he has gauze stretched and taped over his heart, which beats stubbornly independent again, no longer on bypass, the hole mended, the pipes extended. But too big for his body. His heart is still open.

Open heart. In that moment, I saw the mischievous monkey from the story again. He was all grown up, though his smile was as mischievous as ever. He had a scar on his jaw from the thunderbolt that had nearly killed him as a kid. He's been called Hanuman since then. The name means "the one with the broken jaw." Held his chest open, his heart on display. Inside his heart were Sita and Rama, the divine couple, shining with love and wisdom. His heart was full, no room for doubt or fear.

But doubt and fear have crept into the ICU room, demons circling our family. We put up our defenses. Prayers: Pandit Jasraj singing hymns on my mom's old iPod. Positivity: we talk about what Shiv will do when he wakes up. And love: his twin brother stroking Shiv's foot with a little finger. His parents whispering into his ears, touching foreheads to his. Grandparents bringing food, giving support. Our sisters holding our hands. Nurses and doctors working miracles every day. And Shiv fights. Immobile and sedated, he wages battle. Every heartbeat is a victory. Every homecoming is a celebration.

When Shiv comes home from his third open heart surgery, he is a little over one year old. He's quiet. He sits in my lap, looking at the toys and books scattered around the room. Even his twin doesn't try to play with him. Suddenly, he pushes out of my lap, and crawls to a blue rocking horse with a yellow mane. He pulls himself up by the horse's ears and swings a leg over the orange saddle. His face is serious, maybe a bit determined. We watch as Shiv rides his rocking horse like he had to leave town by sunset. Go, Shivvy, go! He's riding for the horizon, chasing that sun, leaving surgeries and hospitals behind. Go, Shivvy, go!

And he does go. Shiv goes on nature walks and expeditions to the zoo. He plays ball with Savya and neighborhood friends. He discovers toy cars and planes. He learns to read and travels into worlds of books and stories. School, playground, parks, and libraries. Go, Shivvy, go!

In between Shiv's adventures, there are routine cardiology visits, echocardiograms, EKGs. Just enough to remind us that what we have is precious.

But then, from the clear skies, another thunderbolt.

How can you ever trust a blue sky again when you've been hit by a thunderbolt?

A cardiac catheterization. The hourly phone calls again.

"He's still in the cath lab. Everything is going fine."

"He's still in the cath lab. Everything is going fine."

"He's still in the cath lab. Everything is going fine."

And then, the last phone call, different again:

"There's no blood flow through his right pulmonary artery."

"What?"

"There's nothing there. His right lung no longer functions."

"What do you mean, no longer functions? Can you stent the pulmonary artery, can you place a conduit? Isn't there a surgery that can—"

"No, there's nothing. There's nothing there."

This thunderbolt is the worst yet. The others had been setbacks. They knocked Shiv down, but he could get up and fly again. This one forever changes the trajectory of his life. Could he fly with a single wing? Could he thrive with a single lung?

When Hanuman was lifeless in the cave, the wind God's grief made the air stop. No breeze lifted pollen from flowers. No current tilted a crow's wing. No wind brought rain clouds.

The Gods begged the wind god to emerge from the cave.

"Not without my son's life," he said.

So Brahma, the Creator, gave new life to Hanuman. The wind carried his son out of the cave, the little monkey rubbing his eyes and waking up. But the Gods weren't done. They each came forward to bless him.

"I give you unparalleled strength."

"I give you piercing intelligence."

"I give you love and devotion."

And so, the monkey with the broken and mended jaw, Hanuman, became stronger and smarter than ever before.

When Shiv lost his right lung, I wanted to yell at the universe.

157

"He has one functioning lung. Where are the Gods? Where are his boons?"

But Shiv never asked that question, even as he grew up with his physical limitation. Once, in the ICU a few years ago, he asked me, "Mommy, am I tough because of what keeps happening to me?"

He didn't ask it to brag. He was just wondering.

And that's when I realized that he *had* been given boons. The Gods were blessing him all along.

Hanuman has blessed Shiv with strength. He helped out his fellow open-hearter. Those … those procedures, those infections, those surgeries? Each time, Shiv was blessed with the strength to fight through recovery, pain, and fatigue.

Vishnu has blessed Shiv with love and empathy. That time his heart had swelled up? It left him with the biggest, most generous heart. This kid will thank each person who comes to poke him and draw his blood. Every time. With a genuine smile. He's always thinking about everyone around him. He has an uncanny ability to pick up on the emotional state of those whom he loves.

Saraswati has blessed Shiv with intelligence and a way with words. Those years of rising above physical difficulty? Those exercises in retreating into the fortress of his own mind? Through those times, Shiv cultivated his mind, with reading, storytelling, and writing. He just finished his third novel.

Considering his childhood, Hanuman's survival is itself a miracle. But here's the craziest part: Hanuman didn't just survive. He's *chiranjeevi*—immortal. They say that Hanuman is around wherever and whenever Sita and Rama's story is told.

When I hear Shiv hammer away on his laptop, writing as if he has a deadline to meet, I know he's forging his immortality.

Live, Shivvy, live.

Through your words and through the worlds of your books.

Live, Shivvy, live.

Through the characters you create and through the strength of your own character.

Live, Shivvy, live.

I'm watching you as you climb that tree, higher and higher, always leaping for the sun.

Twin B

Suss out its source   & a word's a stranger
astronomers   are *star-arrangers*

as if an artist   Ptolemaic
had scatterplotted   night's mosaic

but *amateurs*   are *lovers* of
what's unapproachably   aloft

these scars   we constellate by feel
what lightning scalpels   darkness heals

we're raising twins this way   without
the slightest   formal training how

amateurs blessed   with awe and hope
these double planets   in our scopes

as they arrange   themselves in sleep
with one twin's head   at one twin's feet

as first we saw them   from the ground
stargazing   at an ultrasound

Gemini   jeweled out of sparks
emerging   through the sounded dark

their navels line up   then as now
umbilical bloodbraids   twisting out

to splay & tangle   fuse & tether
this dumbbell nebula together

they float up   through the open window
they thread the oak trees   passing into

the night that knows them   takes them back
to house them   in the zodiac

we chart their hearts   astronomers
of pulsars   artless amateurs

we lie on our backs   observe the ascent
of what is far   beyond our ken

until we wake   to messy heads
nuzzling cozily   in our bed

up with the sparrows   at five past seven
come down with morning breath   from heaven

YOUR BIRTHDAY IS NOT exclusively yours. When it's time to blow out the candles on the Oreo ice cream cake, Twin B adds his breath to your breath. The flames stretch taut and snap into slack smoke.

The first time we saw you together, it was on an ultrasound screen. The ultrasonographer, by a bit of deft wristwork, managed to get you both in a single frame. We saw you both in real-time, divided by a membrane luminous and two pixels thick. A recognizable hand rose and fell, and at first, naturally, we fancied he was waving hello. Then we noticed his hand's movement stopped short each time. A shift in the probe's angle revealed what he was doing: he was tapping on the partition between you. He was getting your attention.

Your brother has stayed in the background of this telling. He has been the one who played with you in the long waiting rooms, who helped you pick out your after-appointment stickers, who woke up with you at 5:30 a.m. on your cath mornings. His omnipresence in your story has tricked me into having him go without saying, like the air.

He was there long before he understood what it was he was there for. The second time you came out of anesthesia, after the major May repair done by Dr. Hennein, we called home to say you had finally woken up. Your grandmother said she knew already: your twin had just broken off his nap, intensely distressed, shrieking for no reason. The shock of your bedbound awakening (tube in throat, arms immobile) had transmitted by twin-twin telepathy, of which almost every parent of twins has at least one anecdote. You were physically unable to cry and thrash. Savya cried and thrashed in your stead.

We would bring him into the hospital to meet you in a one-side-empty twin stroller. On discharge day, after the Kawasaki stay, he leaned over in my arms, pointing with both hands at the vacated hospital cradle.

"It's not a playpen, baby," I said, but Savya sat in it upright and cross-legged. He smiled at us. It was the image of one shared soul, triumphantly returned to health.

From his perspective, the attention in the house would shift away from him. Every three months or so, he found his brother spot-lit at the center of a fuss—thronged, adored, worried over, like a baby discovered in a bulrush basket. According to the uncanny clockwork of the heart's emergencies, grandparents and aunts flew in from different cities to see his brother, and the cousins on webchat asked how his brother was doing, and Mommy's phone conversations started mentioning his brother, only his brother. I think it would have been natural for him, as a toddler or even when a little older, to feel some resentment. He might have broken something made of glass or hit a grown-up or thrown a fit about nothing at all—just to redirect some of the attention his way, if only for a scolding. At least that's what a child psychologist might have warned us about. But your brother never did any of that. We cannot recall a single instance. The possessiveness reflex never triggered. Maybe it's a twin thing, where his sense of self hadn't differentiated fully from yours yet. We could have been fussing over a wound on his own hand. Attention paid you was the same as attention paid him. Or maybe it's a Savya thing.

That mystical, telepathic twin bond can start out strong early and diminish as the twins grow older. The personalities divide completely into two new cells, both with their separate nuclei, their own circular walls. Our anecdotes of uncanny twinterference all date to your first year of life or before. That bond has been replaced by the emotional one.

The Boston cath was the last one where you wanted your mother first on waking up. Ever since, you have asked for him.

Once upon a time, the Prince of Hearts was sitting on a windowsill in heaven, waiting to be born. Behind him sat his reflection, back to back.

Below him were all these places the Prince hadn't yet visited: a bay in Maine, a beach on Maui, old growth forests in Oregon. All the places looked beautiful—even that little apartment in flattish Ohio! The Prince could not wait to go down and start living.

The King of Hearts, who decides which hearts beat when, cruised up on a cloud. "You mustn't look down so fondly, my boy," he said. "You will fall in love with the world and yearn to go down there—and the only way to go down there is in an ouchy, grouchy body."

The Prince of Hearts looked up at his father, and so did his reflection at his father's reflection. "But I already *have* fallen in love with the world," said the Prince, "with its rains, and its bee stings, and its pizza sauce stains. I want to go be born right away."

The King of Hearts frowned. "My boy, you don't know what you're asking for. Every time you die down there, you forget the life you lived. You don't remember your past lives, but I do! I made all those births of yours happy, with nothing but good books and good health. This was wrong of me since there are minimum quotas for sickness and sadness. Now I fear we're up for review, and I will have to schedule you for a fair amount of the bad stuff—and it won't be all red sauce and raindrops, I fear."

The Prince of Hearts really had forgotten all his perfect past lives. He tilted his head, reflecting; his reflection scratched his chin.

"Even worse, my dear Prince, once you get born, you long to come back up here to heaven, every time. What a fool's errand it would be for you to be born now!"

"But I love the world, and I would love a body," said the Prince stubbornly. "Even if it's one with a pebble in its heel, and an eyelash in its eye, I'll take it."

"But what if it's a body with wires in its chest? A body with a whole football field's worth of run in its legs, but only twenty yards of breath?"

This scared the Prince of Hearts, and he shook his head no. But his reflection cried out, "Yes! I'll take it anyway!"

The King of Hearts looked up, startled at his own reflection in the window, and the two of them nearly fell off their clouds in astonishment. The King of

Hearts snapped his fingers twice. The Prince's reflection swung his legs around so he was sitting on the same sill as the Prince!

For the Prince's reflection had never taken birth before—the new body always had its own reflection on earth, while the Prince's heavenly reflection waited up in heaven.

"I'll take all the fevers and all the needle sticks," the reflection volunteered. Though he wasn't a reflection anymore—he was now the Prince's twin. "I'll work through them starting the moment I'm born, I promise. Just so long as I can get held by a mom, and tickled by a dad, and practice free throws with a brother, and get climbed all over by a kid sister."

The Prince of Hearts embraced his new identical twin with joyful tears. "My brother, my mirror image, my self! I promise to crawl every morning into the same bunk as you, even if you're asleep and annoyed with me. And when the needle sticks your arm, I'll handle the fainting."

And so the deal was made. The King of Hearts folded and shaped two hearts, one heart deliberately just a tiny bit off—and he set them beating, lub dub, lub dub, synchronously in the same womb. Those twin boys would grow up to be Princes of Hearts: Their mom's heart and their dad's.

But the things the King had warned about—those things had to happen, too. They started happening, sure enough, from the very first day, and they started with that tiny offness of the one twin's heart.

This is that heart's story.

Twins start out as two souls among the millions of souls circling the world each day like tropospheric winds, all of them in search of bodies. These two souls recognize each other out of the crowd. They might have been brothers in antiquity, or best friends during the Great War, or both.

One says to the other, *Hasn't gotten any easier down there.*

The other says, *Why don't we do this as a team?*

And so, on the count of two, they charge through the door of life, guns out and covering each other's backs.

Unless everything works more bureaucratically, and the souls have to request two forms and appear at a special office a few galaxies over. The forms are in duplicate, and they have to check a box for *Identical* or *Fraternal.* They have to sign an agreement to lock arms and stand fast in the event of a whirlwind. And then they are taken to a back office on the dark side of a strange moon, and there, at the bottom of a lunar sea, is a table with a glass on it. The glass is full of liquid shadow. They know without being told that this is the suffering every soul has to drink down before birth. Once the soul is in a body, it has to cry or bleed this suffering out. Every single soul gets a shot glass full—bottoms up, pound the table, and scrunch the eyes. But their twin birth is of two souls at once, so two lives' worth of suffering requires this taller glass.

You boys were supposed to portion it out equally: one twin was supposed to sip, and then the other. But your two souls rushed the table, and your soul was quicker than your brother's, and you snatched up the glass first and drank it all down. You drank it so fast that the liquid shadow dripped over your chin and burned a thin line down your breastbone. By the time your brother wrested the glass out of your hand, there was very little left.

This wasn't how it was supposed to be, said your brother.

This is how I want it to be, you said. *This is how it is.*

Life and death and new life hook into one another. They comprise a circulatory system.

In this circulatory system, death is the heart, where our lives collect and are sent out again. Blood cells are in the heart so briefly they don't perceive it as more than a small provincial rail station, too small to make the great express train of the blood stop for very long. It's the same way with how our lives perceive death. Immediately on arrival, the blood cells are sent out again to the lungs of this circulatory system. In the lungs, they slow down and oxygenate. Blood cells never actually touch the infinite space outside the body, separated by the thin, porous membrane of the capillary.

It's the same way with our souls and the infinite source of our being. In the interval between birth and birth, we dwell, for a heartbeat, in the presence of the infinite. We soak up something of infinitude and remember it later, in the finitude of our embodiment. Once embodied, we know it as love.

The moment in the lungs, in the presence of infinitude, does not last long. Our lives pass back to the heart, which is the same heart as before. Only the heart isn't death anymore, it's birth, because birth and death are just names for the same thing. And so our souls are pumped out into the world. Embodied, we are meant, like blood cells, to give up what we have taken on. Just as blood cells render up the oxygen they are only the bearers of, we render up our love. By loving each other, we oxygenate the world.

Having a twin is a blessing, a consolation. But Twin B is also an image of yourself with different luck. For everything you can't do, you have a *doppelganger* right there next to you, doing those exact things. Imagine anyone suffering anything—a broken spine, leukemia, a death in the family. What if that person could see footage of their own life as they might have lived it without that catastrophe? What if that person had that film always playing beside them, in real time? *This is how I would look right now, if things had been different. This is how I would be running right now.*

Imagine, too, not just seeing but loving that double, that otherself. The love is total. But the unfairness isn't something you can distract yourself from. It comes up, and has been coming up, in thousands of ways, beginning with the rooms where you spent your first days in separate wings of the same hospital. Lives that should have been parallel diverged utterly and have kept diverging.

Before you were born, your grandparents added a sunroom (a "*grandson room,*" they liked to call it) to the back of the house in Cleveland where I grew up. Your grandmother used to dump out a big crate of old toys I had played with as a kid—chipped Hot Wheels, a fake rotary telephone whose original you've never seen an example of, slack-hinged minor Transformers whose names I've forgotten. She would time travel in her mind, rewind a quarter century as she watched you both in that abundant daylight. A garden swing replicated the feel of the homes of their own childhoods in Gujarat. Many pasts intersected in that one room. One day, when we were all sitting in the mess of old toys, Savya pulled up on one of the legs of the swing, bobbed a bit, and took three deliberate steps to grab a wiffle ball. His first steps! Our whole family converged on him, hugged him, rushed to get the phone to see if they could record him doing it again. I remember keeping an eye on you. You sat and watched the commotion, bewildered. Too young for envy, or for sibling rivalry, you had to figure out what you were left out of.

This is going to be a problem, I remember thinking, *when he's more aware.*

You wouldn't take your first steps until weeks later. The delay matched the exact number of days you lay unconscious after your surgeries. I entertained a vision of you going through life with this slight lag. Whenever life advanced for your brother but not for you, *Wait twenty-three days,* I would promise. But the spread kept widening as procedures and recoveries kept coming. Savya lost his first tooth, and then his second. You tongued your own set, desperately scanning for a loose one. Your body was already stubbornly smaller, and now the baby teeth would not let go of you. I caught you testing them, toggling them with your fingers in the mirror. You lost your first tooth eventually, of course. But by that time, you had registered that your brother was "ahead" of you. That feeling of estrangement from your own body, of wanting it to hurry up and grow already, that feeling of being left behind—you were experiencing it for the first time, but not the last.

In those first four years, the only philosophical thought my mind experienced was bewilderment. Come again? Come again? If I have written any of this as if I really thought or examined these things in real time, that is a lie my memory is telling me, a fiction for the sake of nonfiction. My brain, like the bypassed heart in its ionic bath, lay stunned.

The word *revenant* means, etymologically, someone who comes again.

I return to you on that long dark night of your soul, and I see you ghosted by the light of the vitals monitor. Your mother from years ago is holding you from years ago, in the rocking-chair, in a jungle of wires, while I kneel beside her.

On this visit to the past, though, your twin brother is with me. I am there, inside that scene, but I am also observing it through a memory-window, with thirteen-year-old Savya beside me, Savya at the age he is now, as I am revising this, Savya who plays German Baroque music on his violin all afternoon and loves math so much he has skipped three grades in it and stands almost as tall as I am.

Your mother and I were ghosts until this moment, I tell him. We were insubstantial, see-through, not really there. These are the parents you know because there's finally something about us to know. We used to be ghosts of our future selves.

Maybe that is unfair to us, but it's how I feel now. Your mother and I were never silly. We were twenty-eight-year-old children. We had tried to shape ourselves by reading and thinking and loving each other, but we were unfired clay.

Can I hold him? Savya's voice has changed from his six-year-old voice. He was six years old when I first tried to write about him. He is fifteen now, and like his mind, his voice has deepened. He is early-wise as only a sibling of illness can be.

In this memory, which is really a daydream, Savya passes from the daydream into the memory, slipping across the invisible partition, the chorionic membrane between remembered and imaginary, those twins of the mind. He touches his mother's shoulder, and she looks up, not startled at all. The me from sixteen years ago rises to his feet, and even though the long-ago me stands at his full height, your brother stands taller than me then or me now. He is, like you, growing relentlessly into a man. The long-ago me gazes up at the future him.

Savya slips his hands under his baby twin expertly, one behind the diaper and the other to steady the head, as if he has been doing this his whole life, doing this more confidently than the new father who watches a familiar stranger hold his twin in his arms, careful with the tubes. Newborn Shivvy in the knit rainbow cap doesn't wake up in the transfer. You, too, eyes shut, are dreaming your brother fifteen years from now or remembering your brother from one life before. The me from right now backs out of that unit room from long ago. Savya is with you. You are in steady hands.

Three

FIVE SENSES, FIVE FINGERS, five stresses that comprise a Shakespeare line, five inherently mystical because it's prime, five sections in this book. Two for twins, two for the rhyming chimera of a prosimetrum. But it's three that numbers the dimensions. It's three whose square equals the nine gestational months—and the number of subsections in each section of this book. It's the third that has made this family complete.

A memory: we are in a dark ultrasound room, same as the ones you are familiar with, only this time, it isn't you on the bed but your mother. The clear jelly smears her stomach. I call you boys over, and my lap feels overfull with you; for the first time you two feel like you're spilling over.

You tell your mother not to worry. It won't hurt. You know all about these scans: you had one just a week earlier, a cardiac echo that showed your heart diligently at work.

The probe descends to her skin, and on contact the screen before us crackles alive with silvers and glitter-grays, as if your mother were the source of this electricity. The blurs and sweeps resolve into an image. Thin boxes of vertebral white, the pixelated walnut of brain.

Three is the mystical number, even here. Giving you boys a baby sister was a decision that carried risk. The same aperture we let joy through might be taken advantage of by grief. I warned your mother that we would be opening ourselves up to both. And she said, *I know.*

I warned her that the probabilities were against anything going wrong with a third child, but we could not trust the probabilities. If we had learned one thing, I warned her, we had learned *that.* And she said, *I know.*

We are opening ourselves up, I warned her, because happiness is promised no one. We will be adding a third thing to fear the loss of: we will be creating someone out of nothing, and we will need that person to be happy for us to be happy. If that person were a stranger, and someone gave you the choice to meet him or her and be bound forever after to his or her wellbeing, you would hesitate. You'd say, Hold up, the four of us have made it to happiness right now by the skin of our teeth, and if you link our happiness to a fifth person, and a newborn at that—it's just too many variables! We're almost certain to throw off our precious, precarious happiness.. . . .

"So you really want to risk this?" I asked.

"You want to risk this too."

"I know."

Turn to that screen now, its night sky dense with galaxies. Scan those fleeting white pixels for news of the future the way soothsayers used to read the flight of birds across the sky. Her parents will name her Aishani, but all the nicknames will come from her five-year-old brothers: Skoko, Hono, Bee Scree, random syllables that felt right and caught on, that mean nothing to strangers but conjure those early years for those of us in the know. Eager to belly-laugh and get belly-laughs out of her audience, headstrong, garrulously freestyling whenever she gets a hold of the phone camera: but also preternaturally sensitive, extemporizing on a walk around the block, at age six, a slant-rhymed quatrain that would go on to be published in a print literary review, snapped up by an editor who saw it when I posted it on Facebook.

> Lily of the valley,
> Lily of the moon,
> Lily of the plains,
> Lily of my mood.

The family life that seemed so hectic with two children has come to seem, in retrospect, dull and quiet. Only now that she's here are our lives lively.

Her arrival marked the break that put those early years in the past. One phase had finished, and another had begun. I had enough distance to point and describe. I began testing out how to write this letter to you when she was a year old. She is ten now. It has taken me nine years to shape this into something I can show you and Savya—and, in the future, Aishani, who knows that we all drive up to Cleveland for checkups with Dr. Zahka, but isn't old enough to understand the history yet. nine years of failing and trying again at this, repairing the defects, scanning, studying the screen to make sure there was good flow. . . . Usually, I work way more quickly. When you were two years old, I wrote

Partitions in two months and ten days. That novel had twins in it, and one of them had a heart defect, but I set it in 1947, and that let me do it. This book is different, harder. We lived this.

We have seen some wonders together in the years since the procedures eased up and Aishani joined us. At Mount Haleakala on Maui, you walked by yourself to the edge of that sweeping igneous basin. While your brother and I stood watch (and the ladies rolled their eyes), you unzipped boldly and peed, giggling into the crater. On the way back, you tuckered out right away, the air too thin up there for a single lung. So much swagger, followed by so much vulnerability. So I knelt and gave you a piggyback ride to the car. You were no burden at all, a boy of balsa wood and kitepaper. My steps felt, if anything, bouncier. "Sunglasses," I said every so often, and you reached around and pushed them back up my nose. That remains my favorite hike—your light body clinging to my torso and your gentle breath at my ear.

When we got back from that hike, the sky darkened over us. The plasma screens in the hotel lobby were full of the news: Hurricane Hector was on the prowl. We watched that four-armed, neon-green monster spin across the blue part of the screen, just beneath the dribbled-syrup islands where we were. This kind of thing didn't happen in Ohio much. I did some quick Googling and had a talk with the hotel desk. The worst we would see was some rain, and even with that, the worst of the rain would fall on the center of the island, where the mountains stopped the heavy clouds and made them pay a toll in raindrops. We were in a crook of the island that wouldn't get the worst of those winds. The waves might be higher and more dangerous than usual, but we weren't surfers anyway. Hector was over a thousand miles away—farther than D. C. was from Columbus, I explained. Nothing to fear.

Unless, I didn't add, it deviated just a little in its course, spun a little more north than the Weather Channel predicted. Unless the storm encountered an unexpected dip in barometric pressure and slid down it, shredding these populous islands to its north. I didn't tell you that because I knew that this *probably* wouldn't happen. But that *probably couldn't* implies a *possibly could*. That sense of something always lurking is how we go through life. You always have a Hurricane Hector somewhere south of you. Which is why there is never any point when we can sit back and say, "That's it; that's the whole story."

Proof: I have ended this telling more than once. I have typed some last sentence and decided that yes, this is over, this is all I have to say to Future Shiv about this stuff. But your story keeps writing itself, tenaciously, always another episode. On our next vacation, exactly one year after Hurricane Hector passed our family by, a different storm hit you and you alone—this one without any alerts sent out on the phones, without any storm tracking on the screens. Out of the blue, out of the unexpectedly clear blue skies of the Pacific Northwest.

When Mount Saint Helens erupted sideways in the early 1980s, the volcanologist observing it on a nearby ridge had no expectation the volcano would tilt its magma shotgun and fire directly at him. *Vancouver, this is it!* His last recorded words. He was obliterated instantly, leaving only his last name on Johnston Ridge, like a shadow print in ash. The landscape, blasted raw, is actually too delicate for the human footfall, repopulating itself with the first twitches and sprouts of life. A squirrel showed up to Aishani's delight and started nibbling something on its hind legs. An earthly life form had colonized that extraterrestrial silence.

Your chest is that volcano, I think now, lying quiet after tectonic, titanic eruptions long ago. But you are that squirrel, too—hardscrabble, finding your way, thriving in spite of the scarscape around you and in you.

Mount Rainier's peak framed itself in clouds just for us, a perfect porthole, just as we were leaving the park. You and Savya posed in front of twin redwoods in the Grove of the Patriarchs. One fallen fir tree had split open, cleanly cut as though by sternotomy, becoming the nurse log that fed five new fir trees. It was a very special date, the sixth of June. Your mother and I started doing some small-scale bickering over a map when you popped in from the back seat with a mischievous, ironic, "Happy anniversary, you two."

We don't have pictures of our drive up Hurricane Ridge into solid fog and fat flakes of snow because there was nothing to see. We drove at five miles an hour the whole way up, looked out into a misty obliteration, and drove right back down, an abyss to our right. You boys kept us regaled with ideas for starting a middle school newspaper. We debated alliterative names for it while I tried to keep the car from plummeting that crucial few feet into the dark green, luminous white abyss. There is always an abyss to one side of us. We play with words, we tell stories, we plan for the future to keep ourselves calm. Hands on the wheel, eyes on the road—but the mind on the words to be written someday.

That was a vacation of long, dark green drives: we went north through Oregon and Washington, into Canada, and back down. You likely remember that crowded back seat better than I do: the three of you going over world capitals (or rather, Savya trying to memorize as many as he could, and you rolling your eyes at him), the three of you singing "Old Town Road" over and over until your mom and I had to issue an order banning it. Aishani screamed "Chinook attack!" and lunged, as far as her car seat would allow her, at whichever twin was stuck in the middle seat. (She had discovered this word, "chinook," and had fallen in love with it, shouting it delightedly every so often—the future extempore poetess delighting in word sounds.) We crossed into Victoria and watched the NBA finals. It was a miracle we didn't get complaints from the neighboring rooms as you and Savya shouted your support for the Toronto Raptors at the top of your lungs. That game came down to a buzzer-beater that didn't go in. Millimeters matter, whether it's a bounce pass connecting between teammates or a heart connecting with a lung. We all lay on the couches, exhausted, as if we had played the game ourselves. We would be in Seattle for the next and last game.

On the way back into the States, I jinxed us. Two days before we were set to fly back, I did a Family Poll: what was the best vacation we'd been on? Aishani voted immediately for the Pacific Northwest because she had seen more wildlife, and animals are her thing. Your mother voted for the Pacific Northwest, too, for the same reason. Savya and I opted for Hawaii. Yours was the last deciding vote. For you, it was the hikes in those blue hiking shoes we had gotten you before the trip. The most adventurous of us all, you had clambered to the top of the root system of a giant fallen redwood, me at the bottom with my hands up, ready to catch you if your shoe missed a rung. You balanced your way along a precariously slanted log, graceful and fearless. On the Oregon coast, you went far ahead of us, and when we stopped at a massive ravine, we saw you on the other side, waving. "How did you get there, Shivvy?" You, in defiance of physics and in defiance of basic safety, had *jumped*. And you had made it. "Pacific Northwest," you voted, and the majority ruled: this was, indeed, our best vacation.

We stopped at an unexpectedly roomy hotel in Washington state and, after chucking our dirty clothes into the washer, we all got in our swimsuits and piled into the pool and hot tub. So what if it was well past everyone's bedtime? I had a giddy sense of unreality for a moment as we soaked. This *was* the best vacation. Life was better and better and better. The jinx had less than twelve hours to start playing out.

The Fire in the Heart

AFTER A MULTI-PLATE, multi-bowl Continental breakfast, we got on the road for Seattle. Imperceptibly, while we were setting the route on my phone, the play noises diminished by half. You had gone quiet. You said you were tired. Well, pool play until eleven o'clock last night and a giant breakfast like that—might as well sleep it off on the drive south. Seattle traffic was supposed to be a pain anyway. We would wake you up when we parked at the Space Needle.

At the parking garage, everyone got out of the car but you. I came around to your door, and you were crumpled into your seat. I felt your forehead and caught a whiff of sick smell on your breath—hard to describe, but unmistakable, something I recognized from years ago as a medical trainee. This was bad. The spry, wry hiker who traipsed along Vancouver's Capilano Suspension Bridge just yesterday—who had been swimming in the hotel pool just twelve hours ago, had been wolfing down Froot Loops just three hours ago—was switched out with a drawn face, hooded eyes, pallor, fever. Our long-distance hiker couldn't walk more than three parking spots away. You put your hands on your knees and took a rest.

No Space Needle. Nothing of Seattle but the hotel, at least for us. We figured this was some kind of virus. I was soon on the phone with your aunt, who specializes in infectious diseases, going through a list of possibilities, checking for a list of symptoms. Neck stiffness would have meant meningitis and a trip to the ER right away. Is Shiv coughing? See if he'll pee, see if it burns when he pees. Rash? Belly pain? Or a belly that tensed up when pushed on? You'd been hiking—did you have any ticks on you?

No, on all counts. This fever had brought no friends along. That made it most likely a virus; you had suffered something similar once or twice, and so had your brother. It usually passed after a good night's sleep and regular cups of water. We could ease your fever with over-the-counter Tylenol and Children's

173

Motrin. That evening, we had been planning to stay in the hotel anyway. The Raptors played the Warriors in the Finals that night and won. You watched it lying on your side. We risked no complaints from the management this time. You didn't make a sound.

We had one more day before the flight. The next morning, you and I stayed behind in the hotel room. Your mother took your brother and sister to the Space Needle on that last day of our best vacation ever—without you. One day, I had thought once, he will be old enough to feel the unfairness sting. This was that day. Your mom texted us a picture of Savya lying flat on a glass floor with a tiny parking lot beyond his shoulder, seemingly suspended, blessed with a charm against falling. Another picture popped up—one of Chihuly's surreal, enormous sculptures that had the wildly fanciful look of ocean life. All it would take was a stone. Why did beautiful things have to be fragile? Chattering on at breakfast, mute and devastated by lunch: fragile.... I remembered a childhood trip my own parents took me on, decades before, to the glassblowers of Venice. Those sculptors shaped hot liquid glass with their own breath through a long iron tube they had to keep turning. If they breathed in, they would burn their lungs away.

Tylenol got you onto the plane, but when we got off at Chicago, I turned around from the connecting flights monitor and saw your face as I had never seen it before. It was as though someone had put makeup on you. All the colors had changed. Your face had gone whitish-yellow, with ashes around the eyes. Your lips had lost their pink except for the vertical line of a split. Your body, leaning against your mother's, rattled in all its bones. I was ready to cancel our last, hourlong leg to Columbus and rush you to an Emergency Room. I had seen— and this sounds dramatic, I know—death on your face. I had last seen it when you lay with your chest split open and the Gore-Tex patch over your exposed and beating heart. There at O'Hare airport, passing the silly food court with nothing you could bear to eat, the floor turned to glass. There was the abyss beneath us.

You talked me out of diverting us. "I can do it," you pled, even though you didn't have the strength or will to chew a second bite of banana. "I'll be fine. I just want to go home."

Home from what two days earlier you had declared your best vacation ever.

Your grandparents came to pick us up in two cars. One car went straight home. But that wasn't the car you were in.

Much like the ER doctor who saw you when you had Kawasaki Disease, the Columbus ER doctor wasn't worried. He said the same thing we had told ourselves in Seattle: "It's probably just a virus." The proof was how you had nothing else going on, that by-now-familiar list of questions—breathing, belly pain, headache—all No, No, No. As the doctor was leaving your room, though, your grandfather, seventy years old and a retired physician himself, proposed that they culture your blood. Drawing blood cultures involved a needle stick, but it was worth it. We got a phone call the next morning from the hospital laboratory, one that answered the mystery of the forever fever. You had a species of Streptococcus in your blood.

The luggage from the two-week Pacific Northwest trip went right back into our car. It was a Sunday; my phone call caught Dr. Zahka in his shed, fashioning a table (he had taken up carpentry in what little spare time he had). I told him all the details—how you had nothing but this forever fever. If you hadn't had bacteria in your blood, he, too, would have suggested a tenacious virus as the most likely cause. But with the positive blood cultures, he came to the same catastrophic conclusion. His first words, as he pulled off his carpenter's goggles and sat down on his workbench: "It's got to be his graft. It's got to be."

That was the last, worst possibility, the unthinkable "diagnosis of exclusion." We would have to rule out every other possible source of infection, lungs, urine, belly, everything. You had to come into the hospital.

I was so fixated on racing to Cleveland that I didn't notice the orange gas light on the dashboard until we were in the emptiness around West Salem, Ohio. *Zero miles to empty*, read the alert. Our trusty old minivan sputtered on fumes into a gas station in a town that time had forgotten, everything ancient and ramshackle, full of a melancholy menacing decrepitude. Three days' scruff outlining my goatee, dark eyed and dark skinned and fidgety and out of place, I pumped us a tank full and got back on the highway, grateful that my oversight hadn't stranded us.

No doubt you remember the IV you got in the Cleveland Clinic ER— the phlebotomist wasn't used to working on kids, I suspect, and you grimaced with the pain. Savya stood outside the curtain, but he could hear your intake of breath. The agony transmitted to him. When he looked around and saw your dark blood filling a vial, the blood drained from his face. His eyelids flickered and drooped. What was going on? I guided his fading body to the chair next to you and blew on his forehead. Your phlebotomist, stressed enough by how he had hurt you, now saw a *second* you tipping over in a chair, just to his left. A nurse brought Savya a wet cloth to put over his forehead. I was about to lay him down and elevate his legs, but he started recovering slowly, though his pale lips still matched his cheeks.

Meanwhile, your IV had been hooked up to a saline drip to keep it open. You looked over at Savya.

"Hey, you know, this IV kind of tickles," you said, for his benefit. You gave a weak laugh, trying to help him along, convince him the pain was not even a memory for you. "It doesn't hurt anymore. I actually kind of like it." Your white lie minimized what you felt so you could minimize what Savya felt. Even then, with the pain still sharp in your arm, you thought of your twin.

Along with the wet washcloth to the forehead, and a little gentle patting on the cheek from me, Savya revived. To this day, we never talk about this ICU stay except to laugh at his Victorian damosel's swoon; and that is a kind of victory.

On a monitor outside your ICU room, I scrolled through a CT scan of your chest. I read dozens of these every work week, but here was my own son's. Your right pulmonary artery—the one that had gotten blocked when you were two—had vanished entirely over the past nine years. It was as if that vessel had never existed. The body digests and resorbs what it has no use for. It is ruthless like that. There wasn't even scar tissue.

Your lungs were clear, though—no pneumonia. Everything else came back negative, negative, negative. The paradox is that this wasn't necessarily "good news." If you had had pneumonia, for example, the pneumonia could be treated, and that would be the end of the matter.

Because the search of your whole body showed no source for an infection, though, the source could be only one thing. *It's got to be his graft.*

The tube the surgeon had implanted in you, all those years ago, was causing your fever. Bacteria had cruised to it, bedded down in its lining, and started multiplying. Bacterial endocarditis in someone who has an implanted tube like yours is a dreaded diagnosis. The bacteria that latch onto the graft can be very, very hard to eradicate. The graft's artificial texture has ragged, microscopic nooks where bacteria can get comfortable and raise extended families of baby bacteria. You had been *seeded*, like a lawn by a dandelion clock.

More IVs, more echocardiograms, a CT, more blood draws, antibiotics straight into the bloodstream . . . when just three days before, you had been hiking fifty paces ahead of the rest of us, scoping out the dark green valleys and picking out the best vantage points. You had stood atop impossible rocks, surveying it all like an old-time explorer. They weighed you. You had lost ten percent of your weight.

The bacteria proved to be something called *Streptococcus Gordonii*, which occurs naturally in people's mouths. Every time someone brushes their teeth, these bacteria get pushed into the bloodstream. It's a normal occurrence, and the body's immune system simply kills them. Your own immune system had done so already, every day. At some point, the number of bacteria had been just enough to set up a colony on your graft. Yet you can't very well tell a patient not to brush his teeth because rotten teeth can send even more bacteria into the bloodstream. Toothbrushing! We thought of all the times we had told you to go brush your teeth, to take your time brushing, do it right, do a thorough job. . . . Infected if you do, infected if you don't. It was always a game of chance. But something so innocuous as that!

In the worst case, if the antibiotic infusing through your vein didn't work, the infected graft itself would have to come out. Your summer might end with an open heart surgery—from Oregon, to Washington State, to British Columbia, to under the knife.

Your mother tells me that once, when you were six, you asked her how she felt when she found out that she was going to have a baby with a heart problem. You wanted to know how things appeared from someone else's perspective. What came naturally to you then manifested, in one small way, a spiritual yearning: a yearning to escape the captivity of oneself.

Everyone who came into contact with you, even the phlebotomist who did your 5:30 am blood draw, got a "Thank you." A nurse brought you a warm blanket that night. With twelve leads and wires stuck to your chest, with gauze taped over four separate needle sticks, you wrapped it close and sighed, "Wow! It's my lucky day!"

That was the front, kind and brave and cheerful, that you showed the dozen doctors from various specialties who came to see you. You even showed that face to Savya and Aishani, and your grandparents and cousins, and everyone you talked to or FaceTimed on the phone.

Your captivity in the hospital wore on. The weekend came and went. Your fever was down, but the best we could get was a transfer out of the intensive care unit to a less noisy floor. For a week of summer, you had to sit there, connected to your IV pole like an old-fashioned prisoner to a ball and chain. Every six hours, another dose of antibiotics; between those doses, knocks on the door, stethoscopes to your chest, conversations by your bedside or in the hallway about you that didn't include you. Your brother and sister came to visit, and you played card games and watched ESPN together—but when the sun started going down, they got to leave.

When discharge finally seems like a possibility, I convince the nurses to let you disconnect your IV and heart monitor. I want to free you up so you can get some sunlight. They make the necessary phone calls, and all five of us head out into the summer you've been denied ever since we got back from the Northwest. Beyond the east exit of the hospital, there is a long lawn lined with trees and benches. It's late, and the sun is setting behind the Cleveland Clinic's main building. It casts its shadow on the lawn but not on all of it.

Discharge will not be the end of this. A PICC line will go from your upper arm all the way into your heart, and twice-daily antibiotics will go through it. The rest of the summer will go by, and this hub of delicate, easily infected plastic sticking out of your body will deny you even a game of catch.

For now, though, you walk out onto the grass slowly, swinging your arms a little, testing them out. We stop and let you go on ahead. Your stride gets more confident. You are crossing beyond the hospital's massive shadow now onto the sunlit grass. The border between dark and light slides down your back until you shine all over. You turn, lift your chin with your eyes shut, and spread your arms, funneling all the sunlight in. The IV and the hospital band disappear for a moment. You'll have to go inside again, but that is later. For now, I want to preserve you like this, hugging what's left of your summer. All of this sunlight is yours.

From garrulous forest hikes to a beeping intensive care unit in a day: never get too comfortable, the endocarditis reminded us. Don't think you're in the clear. You will never be out of the woods.

I will tell no more of the story here. In that room, alone at night with your mother, you asked your first questions about the unfairness of it all, detached for the first time from your own condition—and expressed the anger, frustration, and self-doubt that is only natural. I was not privy to that conversation. But that's not why I will stop telling your story here. Already my account trespasses on your memory. You are old enough to recall what happened then and what comes next. I have written this book up to a Shiv who stands just a few years behind you, so close you could turn around and wave at him, and he would wave back, though smaller and less substantial, like a reflection in a subway window underground. . . .

Memory works with every form of storage but physical pain. You cannot remember your way into feeling Boston's botched blood draw. But everything else? I am writing this for you, so why represent in words what you already possess in images, sounds, smells, emotions? Here, your own lively and hyperarticulate mind takes over. You may well write the sequel to this book one day, and at this rate, comparing what you write now to what I wrote at your age, it will be better than this endlessly restarted, revised, redacted, and restored attempt. Whether or not you choose to write it, you cannot but choose to live it. Who knows where you will take this story from here?

The perspective switches now. My "you" gives way to your "I." What has happened since, what will happen in the future—you will be the authority on these things. I want you to know what happened before your memory starts. You can gain resilience by knowing the resilience you have already shown: learning a language is daunting, but not if you know you spoke it once, as a child, or perhaps, like Sanskrit, in a past life. You are not learning; you are relearning. Endure, transcend, rejoice, seek: these are not things you *will* do; they are things you *have done*. No matter what shocks may come, the grammar and idiom of survival will come back to you. Just read this book and remember the mother tongue you mastered naturally is life.

Life. Think about the life in you that forced through all that happened. What musclebound, swaggering grown man, what Navy SEAL, what decathlete, could endure three open-heart surgeries in rapid succession? Cath after cath? Where you stand, you stand unbroken. Know your past misfortunes in full and use them to boom from deep in your scarred chest: *Aham Brahmasmi.*

I am Brahman. Say it. Believe it. Point to your scar as proof. It is the one-line pictogram that tattooed you in your first year alive. I am Brahman. I am the real, I am a revelation, I am infinity, I am the power that lives in shoot, wing, and water: I am Brahman. Who dares push you around, insult you, mock you? Who dares trespass on your sovereign person? Skinny, sure: skinny like a nail in a nail gun. Let nothing and no one intimidate you. No man, no boy, no task, no pain, no test, no threat can stifle the force that woke up gored with eleven drains and catheters but cried out around the breathing tube. If that sound had been speech, what would that speech have said, spoken by the immortal self of you defying time? That was your ferocity. That was your message to your future self; that was your religion and your war cry and your superheroic secret identity. Two words, in Sanskrit: *Aham Brahmasmi.* Three, in English: I am Brahman.

> Liftoff. Two shuttles rise in tandem
> with tickmark height lines on the drywall.
> Whoever drew a mustache on

my twins spraypainted my goatee
with permafrost. These years are vandals.
They duck into the clocks, they're gone.
Is it kidnapping when they switch
your sons out with men? In the mudroom,
two baritones. I go to check—
who are these guests? Five pizza slices,
cold, and a mandatory apple,
and when they get up from the table
they're even taller than before.
Time is time-lapse photography
rocketing them in parallel
taller than both grandparents, still higher
while Daddy watches from the bleachers.
Houston, I have a problem. Age
is a countdown that counts up.
Their math this year has stumped me—trig,
exponents, asymptote sneaker sizes.
Stop feeding them, I joke out loud.
Inside I think, Stop needing them
as if I could stop needing them
to fit into their matching onesies
patterned with rockets, stars, and moons.
It's only screentime stoops that keep them
from low earth orbit. Stand up straight,
I order them, then think, Okay not *that*
straight, not so straight I have to tilt
my chin to look you in the eye.
My twin sons soar past middle school
and shed their mom and dad like boosters
tumbling into the gulf.
First, baby steps across the carpet,
then training wheels, then running after
the bike with one hand on the seat
then one hand on the grab handle
their first time driving on the highway.
From speed to speed, no need for me.
They're at escape velocity.

The Smudge of Kohl

BACK IN INDIA, GRANDMOTHERS would smudge a newborn's face with a dab of coal-black kohl. Maybe just the earlobe. The custom was a holdover from centuries of infants going still in the swaddling cloth, unexpectedly, with no ultrasound to forewarn and no autopsy to explain the loss. Whatever evil spirits snatched babies within days or weeks of birth would be fooled into thinking this one wasn't beautiful. The evil eye—the envy of strangers and maybe even relatives, or other mothers in the village who had lost their young ones in years past—would be averted. This one has a defect, fate would think. I'll pass on this one. Your mother had her double blessing protected against total loss with this salvific flaw. Without it? Both hearts pumping blood to both pairs of open lungs? She would have taken the health of both twins for granted. What seems a gift because she was denied it would have seemed, given unasked, the default. An alternative might be imaginable, with a shudder of pity, if she heard of something like this in someone else's family. Maybe then, briefly, a sense of gratitude, a sense of relief, of being blessed, protected, charmed. But after that, parenthood would have become mere routine for us, only with twice as many chores to do, twice as many laundry loads, twice as many plastic sleeves to fill with Enfamil, twice as many diapers to check for up-the-back explosions.

Instead, this feeling of being singled out as a family, though forty thousand families get some kind of congenital heart disease diagnosis every year in the United States alone. Your suffering is not unique to you. Yet it is uniquely yours.

And there is worse suffering out there. The old texts warn us all that no amount of "faith" or diligent virtue or even personal favor from the divine is any insurance against catastrophe. In the *Gita*, your mother's dearest scripture, which I translated for her when you weren't yet ten years old, Prince Arjuna, the dearest friend of the avatar, was shown the Universal Form, the divine as the cosmos. What he saw inspired awe, but the awe gave way to terror.

Now that I witness you touching the sky, multicolored
and blazing, with vastness ablaze in your eyes
    And jaws wide open, my atman is quaking!
I can find no support or serenity, Vishnu!

    I have glanced in your mouths with their harrowing tusks
that resemble the fires of time,
    And I lose my direction! No refuge will take me! Home
of the universe, Lord of the devas, have mercy!

    …Briskly they enter your dreadful mouths
agape with so many incisors—
    I can make out their haughty heads
in the mash that is stuck to your teeth!

    The way multitudinous currents flow out
Through their river mouths into the ocean,
    The heroes of civilization go into
your faces perpetually flashing.

    As moths in their quickening swarms
are lost in the shine of the fire they enter,
    The worlds in their quickening swarms as well
enter your mouths and are lost.

In *The Book of Job*, the virtuous Job lost everything on a bet—and he wasn't even the one betting. God and Satan observed Job down there on earth like a mouse in a maze. If Job were made to suffer enough, would he curse God?

Job who did everything right, Job who gave regular thanks
for his flocks and his fields and his children.
Bet I can make him curse you,
said Satan. *Bet you can't,*
said God. And just like that
Satan's fumigation hood descended
on the house of Job, airtight
so none of the cruelty could leak: the gangland

execution of his family while he watched,
the sheep scattered and the sheepdog's throat cut,
weevils in the granary, red ants in the sugar bin.

Where were you, snarled the God in the whirlwind,
when I laid the foundation of the earth?

Here where you left me, Job didn't say but should have,
with all my skin ulcers dribbling
mother's milk for sorrows still unborn.
Stab me in the chest, and I will praise you
as I would a surgeon correcting my heart's
defective love. I know
the moon has a dark side, I know
more candles only mean more shadows,
but grief has floodlit me on all sides,
a shaven lion in the heart of this arena
up on two legs for the amusement of my King.

And Job was given everything back,
but it was a different everything.
Better than nothing, but not by much.
In his old age,
he called the new children
by the old names.

So you see there has always been something profound about suffering. Cruelty or indifference, or what we experience as cruelty or indifference, were not excluded from the earliest, most expansive definitions of divinity. What antiquity showed us unsentimentally, we look away from, wanting the God who is all good. Just today, as I am revising this, I contacted a friend of mine recently discharged from the hospital. Before he got the virus, his God was protecting him out of his infinite love and goodness; when he got the virus, it was God's "test" of his faith; after he had spent twenty days in the hospital, and finally came home in time for Christmas, he wrote me that his God had given him the virus as a gift so that he could see, once brought through safely to the other side of it, how much he was loved. He was thankful for it; he wanted to sit down with me and explain how thankful he was. If he had passed away and left his three children without a father, then God, his loved ones would have said, took him early out of so much love. Or else God wanted to test the family. No matter what the outcome, the motivation was love. It armors their minds against despair and fear but not grief. The mind does not always seek truth; it seeks, more avidly than anything, consolation.

Maybe it is better this way. Towards the end of the *Gita*'s eleventh chapter, Arjuna begs the cosmic spectacle to pack up and go, to collapse the diffraction of navels and black holes, suns and faces, comets and jaws. He wants to see the familiar Krishna he loves to joke around with; he cannot bear the vision any longer. So the chapter ends with Krishna retracting into his human form and standing before him as a friend again. This is what we want: the wise counselor, the ally watching out for us, the friend. But it is not reality, seen whole. Seen as you have seen it when your eyelids shut and you go under.

> *What is it like to be eyed by a God?*
> *To come to the notice of heaven?* Beware the vision.
> He will show you two sides of the moon at once,
> the bright and the dark, one merciless-merciful *must*.
> It was easier, earlier. The ancients were harder than us.
> They could bear to see things as they were, see the whole
> hole of the tusked mouth crunching our bodies,
> revealing the howl as a hollow of air
> we make with our mouths, the same as a prayer.

Our old Indian grandmothers knew this, just as they knew the anti-inflammatory properties of turmeric and the health benefits of occasional fasting. They knew it was important to be pious and observant, but not as an insurance policy against disaster; nor, to their minds, did disaster hide any great message or secret blessing. The brightest futures cast the darkest shadows, and that was where disaster lurked, attracted to too much perfection. It must be warded off somehow, if only for the peace of mind of a grandmother who had seen many things go awry just because. Hence the smudge of kohl on a newborn's earlobe. Hence the old hands grabbing the air around the cradle, then curling away and up to her ears, drawing the bad luck to herself, who had lived enough.

Tools

ALL OF THIS HAPPENED. The question is why. You can gnaw that old bone until you are an old man, and your stomach won't feel any fuller. A good rule is, if it's a question you can't answer until you're dead, don't bother speculating; just be patient. Many people follow that rule happily. You can see them in the restaurant at the height of a pandemic, throwing burgers and beers down the chute, with the game playing on three screens all around them. Many people read a pat answer in a book and consider the matter settled. In the year 2007, in Cleveland, Ohio, a fetus's heart and lungs never formed a connection. Why? Because God willed it. Why? Because of karma. Why? Because the universe is masterless, accidental, and our individual fates are just Post-It notes scribbled on and folded and shaken in a hat.

On most days, I don't believe in a God who micromanages things, but on bad days, I pray like I do. A good outcome means I give him credit, a bad outcome means I must have deserved it. The idea I believed most days, with my conscious mind, was karma. Just keep it out of the NICU, and the idea is perfect. Actions over thousands of past births affect the weather patterns of fate in this one. Sins or acts of cruelty, hundreds of years ago in other bodies, are the butterfly's wingbeats that, following from chaos theory, result in a hurricane of suffering today. Some act of kindness or generosity, by the same token, transfers to this life's account, granting someone kind and prosperous parents, or a transfiguring marriage. I loved karma because it was up to me to endure the upshot of my past deeds—and shape my future by good works in this one. How empowering that idea seemed! Suffering was symmetry. I controlled my future lives.

Now walk that idea away from Twin B's peaceful bassinet. Take it on the elevators, down to the first floor, across the hospital, past the gift shop, up in another elevator now to Twin A shrieking inside a noisy tangle of wires and tubes, like a starving foundling snaked about with vines. Karma seems callous. Did it matter what Twin A might have done in some past life? He was here *now*, in *this* body, enduring *this* pain. His suffering shamed divine will and karmic justice alike.

So chance, then. India named the four yugas after throws of the dice. The current yuga is the Kali Yuga, named for what gamblers call the "snake eye," the single dot, the losing throw. The physician in me knows why you were born with your condition. Genetics had nothing to do with it, since your brother was normal. The defect, like the Kawasaki Syndrome that piled onto it, occurred sporadically—that is, sometimes it just *happens*. No larger idea justifies the unfairness. Science's answer to you is just as callous as predestination's or karma's.

Tough luck, kid.

These three ways of looking at it—that number again—I have, over the years, tried on and slipped off again, three worldviews like hats in a mirror. And this may well be as it should be. Believe in chance when you feel resentment, and the resentment goes away, because how is a roll of the dice personal? Believe in karma when you feel powerless before your own suffering or cold to someone else's—because your every action is taken note of, and you owe it to your (future) self to do good to those around you, to rack up kindnesses here and now, to support the family and focus on your work and survive and survive. Be stubborn: make suffering snap its stick across your back and toss it aside in frustration; grab your boyhood by the handlebars and pedal hard; buckle yourself into your future and drive. Believe in karma and restore your future to your control. But when we wheel you into the cath suite or the OR and hand you over to the nurse anesthetist in blue scrubs and a face mask, and your panic shimmers under the sedative, what use is a belief in chance or karma? Believe in the time of crisis, in your fear or despair, that you have a celestial ally. Speak your prayer in whatever language feels right, feels direct and intimate and understood, musical Sanskrit or mother-tongue English, because a word directed Godward sends an impulse, like a rifle bucking against the shoulder, back into the speaker. The mind absorbs that equal and opposite force and gains strength from it. The power you attribute to God becomes yours.

Any one idea of life is inadequate. Instead of relying on ideas as answers to questions, regard them as tools. I have lived this for years without being conscious of living it. As a radiology resident reading a fetal ultrasound, diagnosing a cardiac defect in a stranger's unborn child, I had no thought of divine intervention, karma, or God. I relied on radiology atlases, not holy scriptures, to guide my report. A scientific materialist's outlook determined my analysis and got me through my workday. A few months later, that same radiologist-in-training became a father-in-waiting. I slipped off my radiologist's outlook like a pair of glasses. It was no help to me when I sought to come to terms with the larger meaning of your predicament. Theological concepts like karma and divine will took on fresh urgency. During NICU vigils, our faith became a tool well-known for helping patients and their families: prayer. The idea I needed as a father was different than the one I needed as a radiologist. I set one idea down and took up another.

Your mother and I don't just explain to you the anatomy and physiology, the dangers and necessities of your condition. We also teach you the Sanskrit prayers your ancestors sang. These are all ideas we are hooking onto your tool-belt. The mind takes up the tool it needs for a given task. Science and faith may seem contradictory. In practice—as a radiologist, believer, dad—I experience them as complementary. One contradicts the other no more than hammer contradicts screwdriver. Human suffering is too vast, and human experience too diverse, for any one outlook to comprehend it all.

The pursuit of a *why* may well be futile. Why you? Why your pulmonary artery? Why the complications? We might be turning a rock around and around, waiting for it to serve as a prism. What happened may be just a dense, jagged meteorite that will let no light through, impenetrable.

Even if cross-legged meditation on a mountain and scriptural study and some clinching climactic vision could help you understand your suffering, even if your suffering turned out to fit into the universe like a puzzle piece, would that make it any better? You haven't had your last cardiac cath. It's possible haven't had your last sternotomy, either, or your last PICC line: we must be ready for the unforeseen, as we learned on the drive to Seattle. Explaining suffering and enduring suffering are two different things. Use that to your advantage. Just because you can't explain it doesn't mean you can't endure it. If I could choose between explaining suffering to you and equipping you against it, I'd choose the latter. Wearing a Kevlar vest is better than knowing the physics that guide the bullet.

Remember you are not alone. You will go under alone, but you will never *be* alone. When the anesthesiologist pushes the plunger, you will close your eyes at the center of a crowd: parents, grandparents, brother, sister, aunts and uncles, cousins, and others outward in love's radius. When you open your eyes, texts will light up dozens of phones on two continents. Since before your birth, you've had a brother-in-arms, Twin B. You will be cared for, too, by a whole team. Thousands of brains and hands will coordinate your care, right now and going back in time, all the way back to the first surgeons in ancient Sumeria lancing an abscess or stitching a cut. Just when it feels like freefall, a bridge of hands will emerge from the darkness below you. They will pass you across the abyss.

Don't focus on your bad luck, focus on your good luck. Everyone has some of both. If you had been born twenty-five years earlier, there wouldn't have been a surgeon on earth yet with the technology and skill to fix you. You would have turned blue and passed away within days, maybe hours, of your birth. You could have been born where there were no NICUs, no cardiopulmonary bypass machines, and no artificial conduits made from a mother heifer's neck vein. Every backyard game of touch football followed by pineapple pizza—that day when you were six years old and met your newborn sister—none of that would have happened, if you hadn't been lucky. A chance conjunction of geography and medical history placed you right where you needed to be to survive and love and be loved.

And, finally: *Love who you are.* If you could meet an alternate version of yourself without your condition, you would not recognize that person. Savya wouldn't recognize himself, either, not knowing what it was like to feel faint when witnessing his brother get a blood draw. Your mother and I, too, would have been different people. I imagine that alternate couple's happiness with envy—but also with mild contempt. How shallow, I think, that other us would have been, how complacent, how silly!

Love who you are the way we love you. When you take that first hot shower after getting home from the hospital, look down with pride at your sternotomy. That wound doesn't just show the world that you suffered something. It shows the world you healed.

Once upon a time, there was a boy who was hungry for air. All the other boys ate mac and cheese off the kids' menu at chain restaurants, and Goldfish crackers in the back seats of minivans, and elephant ears at county fairs. Dusted with powdered sugar, red-lipped from a second popsicle, they grew ever more clown-faced, ever more round-faced, year by year by year.

But this one boy would go up two flights of stairs and then lean forward, like he was getting his face close to a blueberry pie. Only he would take big bites of air. Chomp, chomp, chomp, he would eat all the air he could find, and he was still hungry for more. He tried running laps with the other kids in gym class, but he stopped and ate more air instead. He played backyard football, but even when they made him official QB, he had to call time out for an air snack.

With all this air-eating, he grew lighter and lighter, skinnier and skinnier, until he was capable of clambering onto a breeze and sliding across its whimsically curving, perfectly level slide.

What fun he had showing off to the other kids, who had eaten way too much cheesy beef and beefy cheese to surf the whooshes he was surfing! *You are what you eat*, went the saying—and look at this, he was air now! Though quite tough at his struts and hinges: a boy built like a titanium nightingale.

Spoonloads of sludge and forkloads of roughage chased him, but he was higher than his parents now, higher than any forklift or downtown crane. He scooped the wind to his mouth as his body's hollows whistled by. The boy who ate air explored his smorgasbord of sky, growing skinnier and skinnier the more richly he dined.

He has gotten faster and faster, too, since he weighs the wind down less. His parents rush to the windows when they hear the windchime, but they never catch a glimpse of him. "That's just our boy again," they say with wistful smiles, "playing hide and seek." He still visits the neighborhood's backyard football league on a lucky Tuesday afternoon, and he's always the first to be picked. All the QB has to do is hand it off to him, since none of the defenders can keep up. Earthbound, they grab at his heels as he breezes past. He is already in the endzone. So light, he's transcendent. Beyond them all.

"My One Thing"

YOU'RE ALREADY WAKING UP early in the morning to hammer out story after story on your Chromebook. Not too many thirteen-year-olds get their first submitted story accepted for publication in a print literary review. I read your work, and you're writing at a far more advanced level than I was at your age. If this is him at thirteen, I think, what's he going to be writing like at twenty-three? At thirty-three?

This piece is from four years ago, when you were eleven years old. Your teacher asked each student to write about one special object in their lives. This is the first writing you ever did about your condition, your first attempt at anything like a memoir.

My one thing is a hospital band. Yes. A paper hospital band on my skinny wrist. Every hospital band I've worn during my life is important because to me it represents bravery, determination, and power. To me, hospital bands signify my bravery in going through everything I've gone through because of my heart condition. They are like paper scars from surgeries. They also underline determination. Every time I would go through something hard, I would always try to find determination so I can go through it. They give me determination because they remind me of what I have been through. They give me power because they inspire me to become a powerful person. Never underestimate anything, even a paper band, because you never know what it can give you.

To me, bravery is the strength to go through difficult things, including pain, fear, and sorrow. Yes, I have felt fear. Yes, I have felt pain. But I have been blessed with bravery in order to go through scary things. Although right now you might be feeling like I am Mr. Muscular and Fearless guy, I am not exactly well-built, nor am I immune to fear. But whenever I take a test or have nightmares, I imagine a hospital band because it represents the bravery that I have inside me. Over time as I have recognized my bravery, I find myself taking more risks and feeling braver. It is amazing what one little paper band can do!

Something that I have always felt when faced with a challenge is determination. Determination to go through something even though it is hard. I think of determination as fuel to get you through something hard. Along with bravery, determination is one of the best qualities that makes me who I am. I have endured pain you have never felt. I have been made drunk by medicines that taste like unsweetened coffee with grape. (Which is not as good as it sounds!) How do I get through it? Determination, because sometimes you need to face things that are hard. Because I have shown determination through these experiences, the hospital band also symbolizes the determination that has fueled me throughout my life.

My hospital band is my one thing because it symbolizes the hidden power in me. When I say "power," I don't mean physical power such as being able to lift 100 lbs. I mean strength of character. The strength to bounce back after something hard. The strength to withstand suffering. The strength of ignoring obstacles and fighting back. Although I might get discouraged sometimes, when I think of my hospital band, I feel inspired to be a powerful person because it reminds me that I am a powerful person. A hospital band is the shovel I use to dig up my powers that have been buried under discouraging thoughts. Most people say that the best superpowers are physical. But the strength of character that I have, in my opinion, is the most important power around. When a superhero defeats a villain, he often takes the villain's mask as a prize. When he shows off the prize, you see his power and personality. A hospital band is that prize for me.

My hospital band is my one thing because it symbolizes bravery, determination, and power in my personality. The superpowers that I have are not only in my hospital band; they are still with me, even when I am not wearing one. They are my scars; they tell tales of my history. In short, they are me. They have inherited my courage, determination, and power. Even J.R.R. Tolkien, who wrote, "Courage is found in unlikely places," could have never guessed that courage would be found in a hospital band.

I Bow to You

THE SOLES OF THE BUDDHA'S feet had a texture to them. They puck-ered and creased in different ways on different days. Holy men used to walk barefoot back then. For a long time, his disciples claimed his feet didn't touch the ground, but then some people noticed he was leaving footprints on the dusty Indian roads. This scandalized some of them, but a few bold ones dared to in-spect the Buddha's footprints, which were indeed more lightly impressed than anyone else's of a similar weight. To their astonishment, they saw writing: his feet printed the dust like the printing blocks of a printing press, which wouldn't be invented for almost two thousand years. His disciples realized that an entire philosophy of life could be read there in metrical but everyday language.

Some followers even reported seeing much more elaborate patterns there—bas-reliefs of the great city of Pataliputra, alien ideograms and glimmer glyphs, Gods and demons playing tug-of-war waist-deep in an ocean, the first light that ever twinkle-twinkled, the skeleton of the east wind, as-yet-unbuilt stupas and shrines, mathematical equations that could fold space and stitch the ends together. Others saw hoofprints and pawprints and bird tracks and serpentine squiggles, each pair of prints another unexpected species—all the past lives of the Buddha that evolved to this birth. Even those followers, though, concurred that most of the Footprint Sutra consisted of written words: words that shifted and erased in the breeze or sometimes in the breath of the person bending to read them. Sometimes the Buddha's own foot smudged the letters, making them unreadable at the moment of their printing. Even people who knelt with palm leaves and styluses found it hard to remember the words long enough to transcribe them.

When the Buddha's disciples begged him to press his feet in wet clay, he refused. Doing so would betray the illustrated poem his feet were writing. *Everything is impermanent*: civilizations, Gods, demons, light, wind, temples, numbers, poems, bodies. A page—like embodiment, like time—was quicksand not even the light could escape. Hadn't he taught that from the very beginning? Even his own teaching was impermanent, which is why a future Buddha, Maitreya, would have to be born. The Buddha on his begging rounds composed his consummating memoir, a little every day. He alone knew how beautiful it was, and how true, and how brief. He knew no one would ever read it. He wrote it anyway.

Namaste to the conch shell,
The ocean's house, the soldier's horn,
Namaste to the twins of Rama
In my twins reborn,

Namaste to the symmetry,
Namaste to the snarl,
The sneeze in the hurricane canceling out
Swirl with counter-swirl,

Namaste to leads on the newborn's chest,
To the off-blue toes we kissed,
Namaste to gallons of blood-bank blood
And to the Yosemite mist,

Namaste, sleep that slipped the leash,
Namaste to the dream,
Namaste Odysseus sailing home
On a ship of breath and heme,

Namaste myth and isthmus,
Namaste to the wind,
Namaste to covalent bonds
That crosslink twin and twin:

All I can offer is effort,
Namaste is all I can do.
I bow to the east, and I bow to the west.
I bow to the God in you.

*

It is dark outside, 4 a.m. on the morning of January 23, 2008. All night and after midnight, expectant mothers from around the city have been rushing to the hospital. Hissing or biting their lips, they have been wheeled into overflow rooms, rooms divided into two rooms by a curtain, rooms usually used for recovery. It has been a wildly busy night all over Case Medical Center. No snow on the ground, but the roads are plaqued with black ice. The on-call obstetricians and anesthesiologists have called in backup doctors from beds in the suburbs.

Cold red sirens flash on your mother's cheek as I guide her to the car. Her mother is with us, and I drop them both off at the hospital, which is just across the street. I circle back to fetch the suitcase she has readied for the hospital stay. I wheel it across the parking lot, across the street, toward the hospital, laughing with that giddy buckling-into-a-roller-coaster feeling. I puff breath clouds in the cold Cleveland air just for the fun of it. I am not giving a single thought to your heart defect. No one is. We are all too thrilled to meet you and your brother. The joy is pure. The excitement is pure.

In a puffy OR cap and blue booties, in a full-body gown, I pad behind your mother's bed. I stand behind a curtain, next to the anesthesiologist. Your mother is conscious, and I stroke her forehead. Beyond the curtain, in the warm yellow lamp light, the masked obstetrician has painted your mother's body dark gold with iodine.

The joy is pure. The excitement is pure. I would not change a detail.

The obstetrician's scalpel descends, and a valley opens along its path. Water swells and spills through it.

Gloved hands descend and rise.

You are born.

Acknowledgments

THIS BOOK WAS WRITTEN over almost ten years. No other book has given me so much trouble. Not only did I rewrite and recombine its pieces, the book itself kept expanding as more episodes forced their way in. In the end, that delay was for the best. The book's subject has grown old enough to vet this version. Himself an aspiring writer, he published his first short story in a print journal, the *Alabama Literary Review*, at age thirteen. This book has his blessing, and I am grateful it does.

The story itself describes many of the people I would thank in an acknowledgments page, such as Dr. Zahka and my wife Ami. But this book almost didn't make it into your hands, and without some very key people, it wouldn't have. I assumed the story and subject matter was too complicated and unusual. "Publish" comes from the same root word as "public." This account was begun as a private record for family members only. When I shared versions with a few friends who took an interest—early readers included Jane Zwart, Sarah Arthur, John Drury, and Delese Wear—their warm responses encouraged me to pursue an audience beyond the book's original audience of one. After the *New York Times* Parenting section ran an excerpt in article form, letters from as far away as the Netherlands and New Zealand goaded me to send out yet another version of this manuscript. Between its acceptance and its publication came yet another rewrite. For seeing this book into print at last, I thank Gregory Wolfe of Slant Books—the same editor who, almost twenty years ago, as the editor of *Image Journal*, published some of my earliest poems.

This book was set in Adobe Jenson, named after the fifteenth century French engraver, printer, and type designer, Nicholas Jenson. His typefaces were strongly influenced by scripts employed by the Renaissance humanists, who were in turn inspired by what they had discovered on ancient Roman monuments.

This book was designed by Shannon Carter, Ian Creeger, and Gregory Wolfe. It was published in hardcover, paperback, and electronic formats by Slant Books, Seattle, Washington.

Printed in the USA
CPSIA information can be obtained
at www.ICGtesting.com
LVHW101931080823
754621LV00004B/389